THE
PIED PIPER
SYNDROME

AND OTHER ESSAYS

ALSO BY
MOLLIE HUNTER

TALENT IS NOT ENOUGH
Mollie Hunter on Writing for Children

BOOKS FOR YOUNG PEOPLE BY
MOLLIE HUNTER

CAT, HERSELF

  A FURL OF FAIRY WIND

THE HAUNTED MOUNTAIN

  HOLD ON TO LOVE

THE KELPIE'S PEARLS

  THE KNIGHT OF THE GOLDEN PLAIN

THE MERMAID SUMMER

  A SOUND OF CHARIOTS

A STRANGER CAME ASHORE

  THE STRONGHOLD

THE THIRD EYE

  THE THIRTEENTH MEMBER

THE THREE-DAY ENCHANTMENT

  THE WALKING STONES

THE WICKED ONE

  YOU NEVER KNEW HER AS I DID!

THE
PIED PIPER
SYNDROME

AND OTHER ESSAYS

BY
MOLLIE HUNTER

WITH AN INTRODUCTION BY
CHARLOTTE S. HUCK

 A Charlotte Zolotow Book

An Imprint of HarperCollins*Publishers*

ACKNOWLEDGMENTS "If You Can Read" copyright © 1978 by Maureen Mollie Hunter McIlwraith • "A Need for Heroes" copyright © 1983 by Maureen Mollie Hunter McIlwraith • Both "If You Can Read" and "A Need for Heroes" were first published in *The Horn Book*, in a slightly different form. • "The Third Eye" copyright © 1987 by Maureen Mollie Hunter McIlwraith. First published in *Innocence & Experience: Essays & Conversations on Children's Literature* (Lothrop, Lee & Shepard Books).

• • •

Library of Congress Cataloging-in-Publication Data
Hunter, Mollie, date
    The Pied Piper syndrome, and other essays / by Mollie Hunter ; with an introduction by Charlotte S. Huck.
        p.   cm.
    "A Charlotte Zolotow book."
    ISBN 0-06-020379-X
    1. Children's literature—Authorship.   I. Title.
PN147.5.H86   1992   91-39990
808.06'8—dc20   CIP

Typography by David Saylor
1 2 3 4 5 6 7 8 9 10
❖
First Edition

To Julie Fallowfield
in love, admiration, and gratitude
from "the Lion of Drumnadrochit"

CONTENTS

FOREWORD

THIS BOOK—despite one of its chapter headings—is not a "how to" manual. It is, rather, a distillation to some extent of what has been a lifetime's experience in writing—first as a poet, then as a features journalist, with much sideways excursion into short stories, and plays for both stage and radio.

For more than thirty-five years now, however, I have been a children's writer; and although the pieces that follow draw on all aspects of my writing life, they still owe their genesis to that fact. Some are original to this publication, and stem from a wide variety of experience in running writers' workshops. Others have been selected and slightly adapted from earlier publication of various addresses given to conferences on children's literature—my ultimate aim being to interest those professionally concerned with children's literature, as much as it is to teach the aspiring writer something of the requirements of that subject.

To all those, then, who always made me so welcome at such conferences and who gave me such insight on their own part in the creative process, I extend my warmest thanks. To all who were formerly students in my workshops, I send greetings, and congratulations on the successes they have gained. And finally, to anyone newly aspiring to write for children, I offer the heartiest of welcomes along with my sincere hope that these pages will help to realize that ambition.

MOLLIE HUNTER

INTRODUCTION

MOLLIE HUNTER is one of the most talented and versatile authors of children's books writing today. The range of her writing includes books of many genres; picture storybooks, fantasy, historical fiction, and realistic novels, appealing to children from the ages of six through sixteen. Not only is Mollie Hunter an extraordinarily talented writer, but she can articulate the writing process itself, which was the subject for her first book of essays titled *Talent Is Not Enough*, and provides the content of many of these essays for adults.

If you have ever been privileged to hear Mollie Hunter give a lecture, you know the power of her delivery, the conviction of her thoughts, and her respect for her craft. Someone has said that when we listen to authors all we really want them to do is to reveal themselves, to show us the person behind the writer. Mollie Hunter never fails to reveal herself from the moment she speaks with her slight Scottish burr and delightful lilt of language. But she always gives us so much more; she lets us see into the process of how a story happens.

In one essay, "If You Think You Can Write," she gives sound advice to the aspiring writer and provides new insights for those of us who know children's literature and Mollie Hunter's work. Using examples from her own writing and that of her students, she shows the elements that make for quality writing. Always she emphasizes the story first, for Mollie Hunter is a born storyteller. All of her fantasies have the authentic ring of the told tale, for example. Yet characterization must be inseparable from plotting, she tells us. And what powerful characters she develops in her stories. Her realistic novels all have strong female protagonists. It is impossible to forget Bridie McShane in *A Sound of Chariots*, Jinty Morrison in *The Third Eye*, or Catriona McPhie in *Cat, Herself*.

With one exception, all of Mollie Hunter's twenty-five books are rooted in the history and folklore of her native Scotland. It is fascinating to learn that English was not her first language, for her family and neighbors spoke the Doric of the Lowlands of Scotland. Doric had been the official language of the law and the church until the beginning of the eighteenth century, when English became the accepted language. However, Doric lingered on for many years in the small villages and rural countryside. Coming to English as a second-language learner may account for Mollie Hunter's love of words and "the fall of language," as she puts it.

The Third Eye * is a remarkable novel that draws some of the scenes and events from her childhood life in her Lowland village. In her essay titled "The Third Eye" also, we learn that some of the events in that novel actually happened. One of them was the friendship between Jinty, an unusually perceptive child, and Toby, a little blind boy. When Toby asks Jinty, "What color is the wind?" Jinty replies, "It's the color of the way it makes you feel. . . . A warm wind is gold and a cold one is gray." To his query "How high is the sky, Jinty?" she tells him, "It's almost near enough to touch, in winter. But in summer, the sky is forever." Jinty had promised to show him snowdrops in the spring, but Toby dies before she is able to do so. In a beautifully drawn scene, Jinty brings a bunch of snowdrops to his funeral, which, in Scotland, was attended only by men. Jinty stands at the gate until the Earl beckons her in. Slowly she comes forward and casts the snowdrops down on Toby's lowered casket. Mollie Hunter's

*Mollie Hunter, *The Third Eye*, New York: Harper & Row, 1979.

words make the scene stand out in clear relief, but you are *inside* the grief-stricken Jinty, who has her own way of saying good-bye to Toby. It is a small part of this novel, which revolves around the perceptive Jinty and what she will say when it is her turn to testify to the Procurator Fiscal about the old Earl's death. The theme of this story, that courage should have a witness, is one that had haunted Mollie Hunter for many years until she gave shape to it in *The Third Eye*.

As *The Third Eye* grew out of her recollections of her Scottish childhood, her fantasies are drawn from the native Celtic culture and its belief in supernatural beings from the "Otherworld." In *The Haunted Mountain**, McAllister is a stubborn farmer who refuses to give a plot of land to the *sidhe*. The *sidhe*'s revenge is to take him to the top of the mountain to slave in chains for seven years and then be sacrificed. When Fergus, his son, is twelve, he learns the truth about his father and, with his mother's blessing, sets out to rescue him. It is a dangerous task, for the boy will be tested to his utmost by the forces of evil. Fergus proves that there is no limit to his courage, and his love overcomes the evil. This is a frequent theme in Mollie Hunter's fantasies: namely, that the power of love, even from a child, achieves the

*Mollie Hunter, *The Haunted Mountain*, New York: Harper & Row, 1972.

final defeat of evil.

Another theme that runs through Mollie Hunter's writing is "A Need for Heroes," the subject of another of her essays. Just as Fergus proves a hero in his story and the Earl in his, so, too, does Robert Stewart in *The Ghosts of Glencoe*. "The Scots live close to their past and still identify strongly with its events and personalities," says Mollie Hunter. All Scots know the story of the massacre of Glencoe, which occurred when a company of soldiers was quartered on the Highland clan of the Macdonalds, ostensibly to collect taxes in the area. However, their commander's secret order was that they should kill in cold blood every man, woman, and child in the clan. One soldier, horrified at the treachery of the order, warned the Macdonalds and escaped with a few of them. This is a universal tragedy—echoed in the war crimes tried at Nuremberg, repeated by American troops at My Lai. It takes rare courage to stand against authority for the belief in a higher ideal. Mollie Hunter thinks children need to meet such heroes, persons "with greatness of soul," such as Robert Stewart.

Another belief, so true of her own life, is the axiom that "If you can read, you can educate yourself." Mollie Hunter then gives a superb statement in her essay by that title on the joys of reading, for she maintains that:

> the whole reward of reading [is] to have one's imagination carried soaring on the wings of another's imagination; to be made more aware of the possibilities of one's mind through the workings of another mind; to be thrilled, amazed, amused, awed, enchanted in worlds unknown until discovered through the medium of language, and to find in those worlds one's own petty horizon growing ever wider, ever higher.

In her lead essay, "The Pied Piper Syndrome," she gives the facts behind the legend that suggest that the Piper was paid to lure the children into forced labor as serfs for the Count of Chamburg, who desperately needed workers following the huge death toll of the plague. It is this same exploitation of children that Mollie Hunter sees occurring in books written from an adult concept of what constitutes writing for children rather than writing to children's real needs and expectations. Authors who write down to children in a condescending way, or who talk *at* children rather than *with* them, or who attempt to teach with didactic stories, are all piping to false tunes. In order, then, to ensure that there is true promise in the music being piped to them, Mollie Hunter suggests:

Introduction

> There must also be love for children—the kind of love
> that creates respect for them as people, as well as breed-
> ing empathy with them as they exist within their worlds.

Mollie Hunter's books exemplify this love and respect for children, for always, the child's eye is at the
center of her writing.

In real life, Mollie is a vibrant person filled with
the love of life. She has a quick wit and a hearty
laugh. And true to her Scot's background, she is always ready with a "wee story." I have a friend who
says that when the end of the world comes, she wants
to be sure she is in Mollie's cave, where she knows
she will be entertained.

Mollie Hunter has received worldwide recognition for her writing. In 1975, she was awarded the
Carnegie Medal, the British equivalent to the New-
bery Medal, for her historical novel *The Stronghold*.
That same year she was elected by a committee of the
American Library Association to give the May Hill
Arbuthnot Honor Lecture. Her manuscripts are
housed in the Archives of the National Library of
Scotland, and she is one of a very few women writers
to have her portrait hung with the Eminent Scots of
the Twentieth Century in the National Portrait
Gallery of Scotland. In 1992, she received the

Phoenix Award for her book *A Sound of Chariots*. This award is given by the Children's Literature Association to a quality book that has stood the test of time for twenty years.

Despite her wide recognition, I think Mollie Hunter might be most pleased by a story I heard from a teacher of so-called "recalcitrant children" in New Zealand. "Tough Aggie," as she was known in this class, had just experienced the death of her mother from cancer. The teacher wanted to console her but knew that she would resent it. Instead, she gave her *A Sound of Chariots* with the remark, "Here, Aggie, is a book you might want to read. It won't take the hurt away, but it'll help you understand it." Six months later, when a child in the same class lost her brother, the teacher overheard Aggie giving her *A Sound of Chariots* and saying, "Here is a book, Susan, that won't take the hurt away, but will help you to understand it." Such a response is proof, indeed, that Mollie Hunter pipes real music into her stories for children.

CHARLOTTE S. HUCK

THE
PIED PIPER
SYNDROME

AND OTHER ESSAYS

THE PIED PIPER SYNDROME

EVERYONE KNOWS the story of the Pied Piper.

This is the kind of statement no sooner made than doubted, since the mere fact of voicing it brings home the truth that what has been one's own cultural experience has not necessarily also been that of all those with whom one shares a language.

To qualify it, therefore, the story of the Pied Piper of Hamelin is so well known that his name is widely accepted as a synonym for one who can charm children irresistibly into following him. It's in the world of children's literature, also, that this name is most commonly invoked; and so, for all those involved in fiction for young people, it would seem advisable to make occasional recall of his story—and salutary, perhaps, to question some of its details!

Briefly, then, the little German town of Hamelin had become heavily infested by rats, and the Pied Piper appeared there one day, offering to rid the town of these creatures. *But how did the rats get there in the first place?*

The name "Pied Piper" came from this man's particolored garb of red and yellow, and from the musical instrument he carried. *But what was his real identity?*

The Town Council took up his offer, agreeing to pay handsomely for the service, yet hardly believing he could perform what he had promised—and were then astonished when he played his pipe in a way that charmed the rats into following him towards the nearby River Weser. *What was the secret of that music?*

The rats plunged into the river and were drowned, but the Town Council refused to pay up as agreed; and in revenge, the Pied Piper used his music to charm away the children of the town—but not into the river where the rats had drowned. *Why not?*

At the last moment that this could have happened, the Piper turned aside and led the children to a hill that opened like a door for them. And all—except for one child too lame to keep up with the rest— vanished inside this hill, never to be seen again. *What became of those children?*

There is a basis of truth in every legend, all the easier to uncover if one can give an approximate date to its origin—in this case (as will be seen later) the second half of the fourteenth century. And that being so, the obvious answer to "Where did the rats come from?" is found in the spread of rats all over Europe from 1347 onwards.

The extent of that spread was related, of course, to the toll these rats took of human life—they being the creatures that carried fleas that carried the bacillus of the "black death," the plague that wiped out one third of Europe's population. As a center of the grain and milling industry, also, Hamelin was peculiarly vulnerable to rat infestation. And so now to the questions on the identity of the Piper, and the secret of his music—considering these first with respect to his offer to rid the town of its rats.

A skill many centuries old, but only recently rediscovered, is that of attracting rats to their doom via imitations of their most urgent signals to one another—the mating call, for example—all of which signals are sent out at ultrasonic level. In the case of the Hamelin rats, therefore, it seems more than likely that their headlong rush towards the River Weser was in response to such ultrasonic signals piped to them by a skilled vermin catcher.

But that explanation, of course, still does not wholly uncover the identity of the Pied Piper, who must surely have had yet another role to play—or why otherwise would his revenge on the townspeople of Hamelin have taken the extraordinary form of luring away their children? And one further question. Just what was the attraction in the music he is said to have piped for them?

It would be a nonsense to suppose that this, too, was in the ultrasonic range. But it is a fact that an instrument so tuned can be adjusted to play also those notes within the range of human hearing—as, for instance, can be done with the dog whistle in common modern usage. One can therefore assume a certain amount of storytelling license in regard to the actual range of sound used in the case of the children as opposed to that of the rats.

Yet even granted this means towards whatever end the Piper had in mind, why was this *not* the death of the children? And what actually did become of them?

To find the answers to these questions, we must go back to the death toll taken by the plague and the consequent dearth of labor to work the land all throughout the rest of the fourteenth century. This was a serious matter for a peasantry relying utterly on the annual harvest for both food and next year's seed—but serious, too, although in a different way, for the aristocracy who were Europe's great landowners.

These men, finding themselves left with a quite inadequate labor force, were faced with the ruin of the great estates on which depended all their power and riches. A fresh supply of labor became essential, and to obtain this, they sent out paid recruiting agents. It was on young people that these agents concentrated their efforts, and so one of their attractions may well have been that they were gaudily dressed— as was the Piper. Certainly, however, their chief attraction was that they held out golden promises about the life awaiting these youngsters on the estate of a new and noble master.

The disappearance of the Hamelin children, therefore, was no isolated incident—as is proved, indeed, by the record called the Thuringia Chronicle, wherein is told the story of the children who "ran away" from another German town, that of Erfurt. It is this same record, also, which dates the disappearance of the Hamelin children through reference to a similar incident as having already happened there in the year 1378. And so, if the Piper *had* been playing a dual role—recruiting agent as well as ratcatcher—would not that sufficiently explain the sequence of events in Hamelin?

Foiled of his dues in one aspect of this double role, it seems logical to suppose that the Piper would promptly exact these through its other aspect. And, it should be said, this supposition gains validity from the fact that, around that same date of 1378, the then Count of Chamburg is known to have been holding out *his* golden promises to the youth of Hamelin. Also, the Chamburg estates lay to the east of Hamelin, in the part of Europe known then as Bohemia; and to this day, that same area is the home of German-speaking people who claim to be descended from the children tempted away by the Pied Piper of Hamelin.

There is excitement, mystery, and eventually sadness conveying an explicit moral message in the legendary version of the Pied Piper story. There is a certain charm too, not only because one feels sympathy for the Piper himself when he is cheated of his just payment, but even more so because the disappearance of the children is lightly treated.

They are dancing and singing as they follow him,

and so the natural assumption is that they will eternally dance and sing to his piping. But, with knowledge of the hard facts behind the legend of their disappearance, this takes on a different complexion—the sinister one of children lured far away from home and into the grip of a landowner so powerful that he would be able to exploit their labor for the rest of their natural lives.

There can be no sympathy for the Pied Piper, either, once his role in this is realized. On the contrary, indeed, it has to be admitted that his name as synonym for "child charmer" is quite inappropriate—unless the meaning of this can be extended to cover the idea of one who lures children away with promises that turn out to be false.

What we have finally, then, if we relate all this to the world of children's literature, is what might be called "the Pied Piper syndrome"—in effect, that condition created by all the differences between charming legend and hard reality; "legend" here being synonymous with the adult concept of what writing for children should be, and "reality" residing in the needs and expectations of the children themselves.

On one side of the gap between these two stand the professionals of the book world—the writers, editors, publishers, reviewers, and librarians. On the other side are the children, all debarred by their very inexperience from playing any part in the complicated pattern of effort necessarily to be undertaken before any book can reach them. In the gap itself are all the symptoms of the Pied Piper syndrome. Yet how may one identify them? And how can one bridge the gap in which they lie?

There was a time not so long ago when it was all too easy to put one's finger on those symptoms. We were up to the second half of our own century, indeed, before the nastier forms of prejudice projected at children—the racism, for example, the class bias, the sexism—had become unwelcome features of children's literature, and we had eventually entered on what has now come to be thought of as its "golden age." It is still too soon to congratulate ourselves, however, since there is a subtle form of prejudice existing yet in the fact that children are still never treated as being individuals in their own right.

There is historic inevitability, of course, in this attitude towards them—a progression from feudal times when the mass of the poor were serfs whose children were as much the possession of a landowner as they were themselves. But liberation from serfdom meant that, along with certain rights in law, adults were also burdened with legal responsibility for their children. And since children had no such rights, this legal responsibility became the basic factor giving rise to a tacit assumption that ownership of the children was now vested in their parents.

All ties of natural affection aside, therefore, it was indeed inevitable that most children—in effect, those of the poor—would continue to be regarded primarily as their necessary work chattels. As for the minority—those from households with some degree or other of affluence—they would just as inevitably continue to be no more than pawns to parental ambition. In neither case would they ever be considered as anything other than totally at the disposal of their parents; and so long-standing is the tacit assumption of ownership underlying this situation that, even in our more enlightened times, there is still much of the attitude it engenders.

This is not to say, of course, that individual adults today—whether these are parents or teachers—are not willing and able as a rule to appreciate and make due allowance for the varying needs and capacities of children within a class or family group. But it is very positively to maintain that there is enough lingering of that tacit assumption of ownership to result in an attitude that effectually does not recognize children as being fully human.

As a rule, instead, they are treated very much as a sort of subspecies of humanity, with the manner employed towards them—whether kindly or authoritarian—usually being very much one of condescension. A special tone of voice is reserved for them. In practical situations where they are unavoidably ignorant of much that adults take for granted, this is one that talks *at* them, rather than *with* them. In emotional encounters, condescension emerges again in a tone that regards small people as being capable of only small feelings—all of this combining finally to leave them without dignity of any kind. And without dignity, one is indeed reduced to being less than human.

Let no one suppose, either, that children are not instinctively aware of that fact! And so they compensate for the humiliating effect of it by retreating into a world of their own—one that exists parallel to the adult world, yet is still unknown to it in the sense that, in their world, everyone *is* fully a person, with specific standing in relation to every other person in it.

The majority of those there will, of course, conform to its own peculiar codes and regulations. But there will still be rebels among them, mystics, poets, philosophers, and every other kind of maverick, all mingling to make as great a diversity as could be found in any cross-section of adult society—but with this difference:

The minds of all those in that hidden childhood world are always more receptive, more open to impression than they will ever be again. Yet ironically, although we ourselves have all at some time been part of that hidden world, it is the common adult tendency to either forget or repress memories of our time there, that leads us more than ever to generalize about "children" as a homogenous group; and so to forget that although children are in a stage of growing, they are also in a state of being.

So we have finally most, if not all, of the symptoms that make up the Pied Piper syndrome, and can turn now to the question of how to bridge the gap in which they lie—in effect, the one that asks how we may ensure there is true promise in the music being piped for children.

It is the writer who is considered to have prime responsibility in this, of course, since the mere fact of being a children's writer carries the presumption that one has free passage between the childhood world and that of the adult. That presumption is totally false, however, unless the children's writer is aware—consciously or otherwise—of all the symptoms described above and can recognize from them that there is no such creature as the one conveniently titled "the child reader."

There is, instead, simply a diverse collection of people at various stages of growth; and for the promise of the music to ring true to those who happen to be most advanced in this, there must be at least some orientation towards the adult world for which they are destined. A first onus on the writer for these older children is therefore to waken them to the realization that they will not be able to find the magic of it except *within themselves.*

Humanity has been capable always of extremes in brutality and hypocrisy, yet equally so of sublime self-sacrifice, supreme endeavor. But for the adult world to be truly a magical place for the individual, there must still be more than just a balance between these two sides of human nature. The good side must always positively outweigh the bad; and the onus mentioned is therefore one that calls for the writer to re-create in story terms any of the many possible ways to victory in this.

To do so without didactism—whether overt as this used to be, or concealed, as it so often is nowadays in stories of "social realism"—must also be the aim. Children have always been quick to resent the former, just as quick to detect and resent the latter. Besides which, although one may drag young people along the path to discovering the world, the truest form of exploration is still that of discovering self. And the route to that end, lonely as it always is, is still the sole one towards realizing that each one of us *is* in command of that inner magic.

Fiction for younger children, however, presents the writer with a different set of circumstances—the vital requirement here being that of empathy with the attribute that all these children have in common. One and all, they *believe* the promise of magic in the music being piped for them. But this still does not mean that such children are gullible. Far from that, the belief is there among the shrewdest and most practical of them, and the source of it is not far to seek.

First is the fact that—contrary to popular belief among adults—the horizons of young children are *not* limited. Paradoxically, indeed, it is the very lack of experience among children of up to—say—ten years old, that means there are *no* boundaries to what might happen in any unknown circumstance. Possibility is therefore quite literally endless—and, that being so, could well encompass magic. A further fact is that young children are atavistic, in that their minds revert naturally to the primitive concepts of reality and magic as happily coexistent with one another—something that can best be illustrated, perhaps, from practical experience.

As an eight-year-old watching a performance of J. M. Barrie's *Peter Pan*, I was one of hundreds who not only accepted quite naturally that Peter could fly, but who also cheered on the delighted discovery of the other children onstage that they, too, could fly. And two generations later, in a cinema packed with children watching Steven Spielberg's film *E.T.*, I heard the same excited burst of cheering when the bicycles ridden by that story's youthful characters took *them* suddenly soaring into flight.

When one is writing for younger children, then, to hold in mind this atavism as well as that acceptance of limitless possibility is also to realize how terribly vulnerable they are to any transgression of their belief in magic. But that belief, of course, need not be narrowly defined as pertaining only to matters supernatural.

The fantastic and otherwise inexplicable have their own charm, in this respect. But if one remembers that lack of experience which could make *anything* possible, the mundane world of everyday could equally be transformed by something that is also magical in that it gratifies for the young reader some unspoken yearning, some secret expectation that would never otherwise have a voice.

The further we drift from acceptance of this, also, the greater will be the danger of false promise in the music piped for them, and so the less able will we be to cross the gap that holds the symptoms of the Pied Piper syndrome. And strangely enough, as it happens, it was in the town of Hamelin itself that I once witnessed a real and physical counterpart of that very situation.

It was on one of the days in summer when the citizens of that town mount an annual reenactment of the Pied Piper story. From far and near there were people pouring into Hamelin to see this play, and traffic was becoming hopelessly snarled up. It was a very hot day. From where I stood watching the crowd, I could see a traffic policeman—a very pompous man—who was becoming more and more bad-tempered over the traffic problem.

He scowled and shouted, his face scarlet with annoyance and the heat. On the pavement nearest him were some of the children of Hamelin dressed for their part in the play; and suddenly from among these a small boy darted out to hand the traffic policeman a red rose. I had no idea of the significance of this gesture—or, indeed, whether it had any significance at all. But I could see that the child was smiling, and had obviously offered the rose as a gift.

The policeman did not take it as such. He simply snatched impatiently at it and then carried on directing the traffic, whistle in one hand, red rose waving furiously from the other. It might have been funny to see this—a policeman angrily directing traffic with a red rose as a pointer—and some of the bystanders did indeed find it comical.

I didn't. I was watching the small boy making his way back to the rest of the children, looking forlornly over his shoulder towards the policeman as he did so; and I was thinking then as I still think about this incident.

The whole play in prospect was about children. That whole day devoted to it was a children's day; yet the policeman had become so preoccupied with his responsibilities in it, that he had spoiled what might otherwise have been the most magical moment of it all for that small boy.

In the writing world—or so it finally seems to me—the child needing, expecting, to be carried into some circumstance beyond its own imagining is the counterpart of that child holding out the rose. The complementary gesture—that of gracefully accepting the rose—needs more to motivate it than any of the writer's inherent gifts, more than the skills to exploit these gifts. There must also be love for children—the kind of love that creates respect for them as people, as well as breeding empathy with them as they exist within *their* world. It is only when that final quality enters the situation, indeed, that the hand of the writer can touch that of the child. But here is what happens then!

The Pied Piper syndrome finally vanishes—because those hands touching across the gulf between the child and the adult world, and having but one grasp on the same flower, are holding between them the flower of a promise. And, unlike the one made by the Piper, this is a promise of magic that will not turn to bitter disappointment, of pleasure that will not sour—because that promise, too, is one that has been made in all honesty, and has been just as faithfully fulfilled.

IF
YOU THINK
YOU CAN WRITE

PEOPLE ARE CURIOUS about writers. We all use language, after all, and so how is it that some can do so in a certain way and others can't? What's the secret? The myth that there *is* some sort of secret to be learned is only one of the many surrounding the writing world; but the most prevalent of such myths is still that about writing for children.

Telling stories to children—well, that's something most people have done at one time or another. Lots of them, too, have been very successful at this. Some have even charmed a particular group of children with the written version of a favorite tale of their own invention. And so, runs the myth, to do the same professionally is bound to be pretty easy—

more of a money-spinning hobby, in fact, than a "real job."

There is no short way to dispose of this myth. But not everyone, fortunately, is taken in by it; and among these will always be some who do genuinely wish to be able to write for children. To continue in the terms that could be helpful to them, therefore, it has to be emphasized initially that this is a specific genre of writing, and that writing itself is a pursuit dependent on certain inherent attributes.

In the writer of fiction, also, the most obvious of these attributes is the desire to communicate experience in story form; but before this or any of the other attributes that inherently exist can perform their destined function, the person concerned must acquire certain technical skills. *And all this is as true for the children's writer as for any other.* To pursue the genre of children's fiction, however, means that these acquired skills have to be developed in certain ways; as, for example, in building from another of the writer's inherent attributes—that of the gift of words.

This is where two complementary circumstances have to be taken into account, the first of these being a practical one, the second calling for exercise of yet another inherent attribute—that of imagination. The practical circumstance is that publication of a children's book is governed by more than its literary merit. The reader's assumed attention span is also a relevant factor. Similarly so is the fact that costs of production relate to the book's length; and further, that these costs have to be set against a retail price which is generally lower than that of books in the adult market.

It's true, of course, that children's books of inordinate length have occasionally and very successfully been published; and anyone who is genuinely moved to attempt writing such a "blockbuster" should certainly do so. But to stay here with the factors that generally apply, what these mean for the writer is that the length of any piece of fiction—whether this is a picture storybook or a novel for teenage reading—is more or less dictated in advance of writing; and so, to succeed in either of these fields or in any of the forms between, that gift of words has to be put to very specific use.

This implies more, however, than the fact that one cannot write in a manner such as that of novelist Henry James, of whom it has been remarked that he never used one word where six would do. Quite apart from the need to avoid such prolixity, it is essential also to realize that the gift of words must consist of more than its capacity for enabling one to acquire a large vocabulary and to appreciate the "fall" of language.

To write *well* for children, in fact, that gift must also achieve an ability to compress meaning to the point where one word may have to do the work of six; to do so, moreover, by increasing rather than diminishing the imaginative stimulus of the text. And the younger one's readers are, of course, the more this applies.

The picture book would therefore seem to be the ultimate example of any such achievement; but that, unfortunately for the many who have made so facile a judgment, is far from being the case. The very young child has little or no vocabulary, and the release of emotions through a picture book depends on its projecting an inspired keynote which conveys either that feeling of tenderness (but *not* sentimentality) towards which all young children yearn, or else that gorgeous lunacy that empathizes immediately with their lack of mental inhibition. In the best and most original of picture books, also, there can be a combination of such appeals—both of which are necessarily dependent much more on the artist's skills than on the text linking one illustration to another.

Once the picture-book stage is passed, however, and the child's understanding is dependent more on language than on pictures, the point where imagination builds out from emotion has also been reached; and it is then, in the form we know as the picture storybook, that the writer has to become ingenious not only with words which will appeal to that imagination, but also in supplying the artist with the brief but evocative phrasing that will inspire illustration of the story's highlights.

For example, the child hero in this story is entering "the Dark Forest"—a woodland area of great menace.* But simply to state this "menace" as a fact will not convey to the young reader the foreboding of danger and the sense of fear implicit in that word. These feelings have to be evoked in a choice of words that enable the artist to create in the reader's mind the actual form taken by that fear and foreboding— as was done here through showing the trees of the Dark Forest to be "big, and old, and thick, and ugly," the bark of their trunks crumpled into "the shape of strange and threatening faces," and growing so close together that they surround the small hero-figure with whom the reader has identified, like "a regiment of ancient and crippled giants massed on every side of him."

*Mollie Hunter, *The Knight of the Golden Plain*, New York: Harper & Row, 1983.

Descriptive writing like this, however, must be able to do more than evoke for the young reader the feelings inspired by the setting for some story incident. It must relate also in much more subtle ways to the fact that young children have no frame of reference for some of the emotions one may wish to show as flowing between one character and another. Similarly, they have no frame of reference for what may be to adults the ultimate in physical terms.

What does it mean to a nine-year-old, for instance, to say of a woman that she is so beautiful, no man can resist her? There is no frame of reference here for the inference of the power of sexual attraction, no concept of what to the adult male would be irresistible beauty of face and form. Yet this is typically one of those recurrent story situations where a man is drawn by basic human emotions into the dangerous orbit of power created by the legendary attraction of a fairy woman.

Typically also, therefore, it is one that calls for a subtle use of language to provide that needed frame of reference by creating what *to the child* would be the irresistible attraction to the story character in the woman he found "waiting for him at the grazing-ground, as beautiful as he remembered her. Like a man under a spell—which indeed he was—he went towards her. And like some magic creature *made of gold and flowers and sunshine and music*—which indeed she might have been—she drifted into his arms" [italics inserted].*

So, as indicated, it is this constant refinement of vocabulary that has to take place before the children's writer can satisfy the requirement to write concisely yet imaginatively. Nor does the successful implementation of that requirement impose any shortcomings on the end result as this may be considered in purely literary terms. Far from that, indeed, it is likely to be a much better piece of writing *as such* than would have been the case had there been the unlimited "elbow room" generally allowed in the adult market.

It's in striving towards this point, indeed, that one finds not only the style which suits the text, but which *suits oneself*—a point that was very strongly driven home to me on one occasion by the advice that was the beginning of all my writing for children: "Write what you like, how you like. And sooner or later, if it's good enough, someone will publish it."

Note that caveat—"if it's good enough." It's not only on language skills that a book rests, and it *can* only be good enough if one has learned how to structure the text in question. The shape and sound-

*Mollie Hunter, *The Wicked One*, New York: Harper & Row, 1977.

ness of that structure, also, will depend on two things—characterization and plotting—but ultimately, too, on a third—the point of entry into the story. There are complications here, however, that are perhaps best initially explained by describing a manuscript submitted for criticism by a young woman student in one of my writers' workshops.

The work was the first half of an adventure novel for teenage readers. Its heroine was Jenny, a girl of fifteen, and the plot revolved around her determination to prove her independence by living rough for a month in the Canadian Rockies. The manuscript was well laid out—a requirement of which all too many aspiring writers are woefully ignorant! The idea for the plot was a good one, suggesting the emergence of an interesting theme; and the standard of writing, also, was good. All this was negated, however, by one basic failing.

The girl, Jenny, had no more than surface dimension. She had left home without telling her parents where she was going, without any explanation of her disappearance—this being presented simply as part of her determination to "prove" herself. For all of that first half of the novel, also, there was no further mention than this of her parents, no hint in any way of Jenny's former life, in either its practical or its emotional aspects.

The writer, in effect, had offered the reader no way at all of identifying with Jenny. She was a cipher, someone existing in a vacuum. Well plotted and well written as her adventures were, therefore, there was no possibility of these creating a chiming of imagination between writer and reader. And all this was simply because that aspiring writer had yet to learn two things about the craft—first, that fictional characters must be as fully equipped with minds, wills, and emotions as oneself; and second, that characterization and plotting are and always will be inseparable from one another.

It's true, certainly, that one may conceive a book originally out of either a character or an idea for a plot. The character may be based on someone noted in real life. He or she may be drawn from within some aspect of one's own personality crying out to be expressed. But either way, that character remains incomplete in his or her own right until visualized as being mentally and emotionally as well as physically engaged with some other person, or persons.

The extension of this is that the very manner of that engagement will in itself contain the germ of a story. As that story grows, so will the imagination breed other characters relevant to its incidents. But, since neither the original character nor any of the others will ring true to the reader unless portrayed as beings with minds, wills, and emotions of their own, it is the way *they* think, the way *they* feel that will be the determinant factors in developing these incidents into a coherent plot.

So do plot and characterization eventually mesh to the point where each needs the other to keep the story moving forward; and precisely the same is true of the situation where it is the idea for the plot that dawns first. The characters needed to carry the plot may be based on people noted in real life or drawn from within oneself, but must still be imaginatively filled out to become whole personalities whose actions and reactions will inevitably shape the plot's development. And as before, it is exactly from this meshing of plot and characterization that the story will receive its impetus.

There is no better way to bring oneself to this point, either, than by writing about one's characters *before* the actual task of writing the book; writing about them to the point where they are as real to you as any flesh-and-blood people daily encountered. That means first of all giving each one a name, and thinking always of each one by name—as one would naturally do, say, with friends or members of one's family. It should mean also inventing a past for them, the past that must have existed for them if they are indeed to be so real to you that you will inevitably be able to project them as beings who will be real, also, to your reader.

To introduce them to your readers, however, means deciding on the point of entry into your story; and this, the final task in structuring a book, is unfortunately also the most difficult one. The solution to it is one that can be arrived at sometimes only after much trial and error—but even so, it's in this very situation that all one's prewriting, as it were, can be vital to arriving at a decision. In other instances, it can be the result of an inspired moment when the picture of some scene or other flashes into the mind, and you just know somehow that this is how and where your book *must* start. Or sometimes it can be a combination of both—lots of trial and error; and then, in the midst of it, that brilliant moment when the opening scene is suddenly there and absolutely demanding to be written.

Trust that moment. Always trust it completely. And if it's a scene of action that's held there, then all the better for you. Young readers don't want to be led into a story. They want to plunge into it. But, whatever else you do with that opening scene, remember also that its young readers are likely to have only minimal knowledge of what is well known to you as an adult; and so, even when the action in an opening scene is sufficient in itself to ensure reader attention, it should still have woven into it at least some of the "markers" that will indicate its setting, and possibly also its place in time. Either that, or it should very quickly be followed up by another scene that enables these markers to be placed.

As to the eventual nature of the structure to be built on any opening scene, the most useful attribute a children's writer can possess in this respect is the kind of highly visual imagination needed to bring a stage play alive. To be able to see one's characters acting out a scene, as it were, in the course of the chapter in hand, and then to close that chapter with the equivalent of what would be, in theater, a blackout, is to create a cliffhanger that makes the opening of the next chapter an irresistible attraction to the reader. Similarly, if one plants the leads for this next chapter close to the end of the one preceding it, and then finishes that preceding chapter with the equivalent of a diminuendo of stage lighting, the temptation to follow up these leads is again what draws the reader further into the story.

There is one further advantage in this type of

imagination—particularly when it comes to writing a scene of action. It's something that enables one more clearly to recognize that the factor vital to success in portraying such a scene is simply this: *It should never take longer to read than it actually does to happen.* This is a lot more difficult to achieve than one might imagine; but even so, it's still a technical skill that has to be acquired if one is not to produce the type of descriptive passage which would otherwise tend to be confusing, long-winded, and therefore also boring.

Both for those who would naturally visualize an action scene, therefore, as well as for those who would not so see it in the mind's eye, a basic requirement is to choreograph it as carefully as would be done with the steps of a dance—or, indeed, as is done in the film or theater world when a stunt has to be arranged. And all the better again, if one has the chance to do so in a practical way, rather in what can develop into some totally frustrating struggle with syntactical terms.

To illustrate with the best chance ever offered to me in this respect: I was engaged in writing a book* where I had arrived at a vitally important action scene, when my son—who happened to be a soldier at that time—arrived home with his sergeant for a

*Mollie Hunter, *The Stronghold*, New York: Harper & Row, 1974.

cup of coffee. The sergeant was big, broad-shouldered, sinewy, and cold-eyed—the type of man I wouldn't have liked to meet in the dark with a knife in his hand and a grudge against me. I asked him how good he was in close combat, and he admitted politely to having done "a fair amount" of that.

"Right," said I, producing three pot lids and three wooden spoons, "you're a Celtic warrior armed with a long sword and a small, round shield. My son and I are Roman soldiers armed with short swords and long, rectangular shields; and we're going to come at you and kill you."

The sergeant—as well he might—looked considerably taken aback at this; and then, with a thin attempt at a tolerant smile, accepted his pot lid and spoon. My son—who knew the tactics I had in mind—kept a straight face. He and I also "armed" ourselves with wooden spoons and pot lids. Then we closed in on the big sergeant, and "killed" him.

He was indignant, of course. It's not every day, after all, that a Rambo type finds himself on the floor with a raw young soldier and an elderly woman standing triumphantly over him. But after the dust had settled and I had explained what I was attempting to do, I was able also to persuade him to a careful, step-by-step rehearsal of all the actions involved;

and the scene as eventually written was less than two hundred words long—in effect, the reading time needed matched exactly the time occupied by the action.

There is much more to the business of handling time, however, than is involved in the aspect mentioned. Overall, indeed, it is the greatest single problem a beginning writer has to face, simply because time in real life has to accommodate much that, in fiction terms, is irrelevant and therefore boring. The technique of manipulating a text so as to compress or eliminate these irrelevancies is therefore a basic essential skill, and the first step in acquiring this is to decide the total time frame of one's story. A day, a week, five years—it makes no difference what that time frame is; it must still be there, clear in the mind, before the story it is to contain can be structured.

That decision, however, is not necessarily arrived at in any mechanical way. A book may have a long period of gestation before it finally demands, as it were, to be written—by which point its time frame may already have decided itself. Much of the incident to be developed within that time frame may already also have taken shape. But whatever the circumstances preceding the actual writing of the book, the essential next step in this business of handling time is that of deciding how to *pace* your story—and here, it is the storytelling instinct that comes primarily into play.

That instinct should infallibly alert one to what the high points of the story should be. But to be able to pace these in a way that will hold reader interest calls for the writer to discard everything that will *not* work towards that end. To achieve this means first of all that these high points must always be kept clearly in focus. This, in turn, means deploying forethought not only in working from sentence to sentence and paragraph to paragraph, but also in relating these lesser sequences to their containing chapters, and in leading from one chapter to another; the ultimate aim of the whole process being a text so cleared of irrelevancies that it links each of these high points directly to all the others, and so also gives them collective as well as individual impact.

All this may sound at first a daunting task, but the beginning writer should take comfort from the fact that there is at least one tried and trusted aid towards solving the problem it presents. This is simply to begin by writing a précis of each of the story's high points. The précis can then be expanded into the form of a chapter in which—since everything inessential has already been considered and rejected—there is much less likely to be difficulty with syntax and correspondingly more of pure pleasure in storytelling.

For example, in that book already mentioned, *The Stronghold,* I find in my notes the following précis of a high point provided by the situation in which a principal character, Nectan, has to prove his fitness to be chieftain of his tribe by engaging in ritual combat with its symbol—that of a wild boar.

> Nectan—his bloody triumph in a battle with the boar is convincing proof of his fitness to rule. But Nectan's enemy, Taran, is still not prepared to give up his ambition to be the tribe's chief, and so this must also be the occasion for strong emergence of the women in the story.

In expanded form, then, this high point became a chapter that comprised not only the battle itself but also the reactions to it of Nectan's wife, Anu, and his daughters, Clodha and Fand, also those of his enemy, Taran. So, into what was ostensibly only a scene of action, with the killing of the boar as its climax, were woven all the outstanding characteristics of the three women, together with the plot threads of further action which *many months later* was to involve them as principals in the final struggle against Taran.

In effect, then, the key to this question of handling time—which is also, of course, the key to that selectivity already mentioned—is to be always, as it were, writing *ahead* of the plot, *but without the reader realizing that this is so.* To achieve this means consistently planting the text with leads for the story's later episodes. And to succeed in doing so means that, rather than allowing it to sag like a piece of worn elastic (as it certainly would do otherwise), the writer will have imparted to it instead the most vital of all its elements—that of *tension.*

Be warned in this, all the same, that the skills described can be needed as much in a simple running narrative for the younger child as they are in a book more extensively planned. And be warned, also, that although you are writing for children, you are not writing for people of lesser intelligence than yourself, but simply for those with less experience. You are most unlikely to interest them, therefore, unless you are writing about something that also interests you personally.

The thought processes of children, too, are often considerably sharper than those of adults; added to which, children's interests are frequently diverse enough to make them more informed than adults on certain subjects—both of which considerations give rise to a further warning.

To write about what interests you is still not good enough unless you are also writing about what you *know*. The alternative here, therefore, is to be thorough in your research—if, that is, you are to avoid the kind of error which further marred the work of that student of mine who wrote about no-character Jenny.

This Jenny, you'll remember, was alone in the Canadian Rockies. Her adventures there began with her finding a black bear cub, left motherless after the she-bear had been drowned in a river flooded by melting spring snows. The cub was described as "a yearling." Jenny takes the yearling to her cabin in the woods. She feeds it, pets it; they become firm friends, wandering in the woods together, sleeping and playing together. On one of their wanderings they come across the drowned body of the yearling's mother. The yearling is distressed. Jenny gathers wood, piles it round the she-bear's body, and waits with the yearling till this is consumed to ashes. Happy Jenny! Comforted yearling! But just how plausible was all this?

The black bear of the Canadian Rockies cubs once every two years, the young staying with the mother till she is once again due to cub. Cubs are always born in January. At the end of March, when Jenny found her orphan cub, it could not therefore have been a yearling. It would have been either three months or fifteen months old. If the former had been the case, and even if she could have given it the nourishment it required at that stage of growth, it would still already have learned to be intolerant of human contact. In the latter case, this would have been infinitely more so.

A female of fifteen months, also, would have weighed between a hundred and fifty and a hundred and seventy pounds; a male would have scaled at some fifty pounds more. In either case, even a playful cuff would therefore, at the very least, have stunned the girl—possibly even have killed her. To burn to ashes the body of a full-grown she-bear, finally, would have meant cutting and stacking enough timber to burn at least three hundred pounds of flesh—a job that would have needed the energies of at least a couple of experienced lumberjacks!

It's possible, of course, that an editor might have neglected to run a check on the research required, and thus allowed such dreadful failings in this respect to pass undetected. But even so, if such failings had ever reached publication in book form, there is not the slightest doubt that young readers *some-*

where would have spotted them! My student took this, as well as my other criticisms, in good part; and in return I made no bones about confessing to her that I had once made just as great a mistake as hers—although on opposite lines.

This was when I was writing a book set on the Shetland Isles—one which I had spent years researching.* At the end of six months' writing, however, all I had to show for my efforts was really nothing more than a good guidebook to Shetland. In other words, and in spite of all my experience as a writer, I had still made one of the most elementary errors in research. I had let the results of this *show*, instead of—as I should have done—allowing them to sink into my mind until they became so integral a part of my thinking that, simply as a matter of course, I would have woven them unobtrusively into the story only as and when this needed to be done.

I wept bitter tears over that wasted six months' work, tore it all up, then started afresh; and I'm glad to say the book that resulted is still going strong. I'm even happier to say, however, that some time after my workshop finished, my student took the trouble to seek me out to let me know that she had, at last—and successfully—published *her* book.

To recapitulate, then, in terms of this same stu-

---

*Mollie Hunter, *A Stranger Came Ashore*, New York: Harper & Row, 1975.

dent, it was possible for me to teach her something about writing for children only because she was one of those inherently gifted *as* a writer. Quite apart, also, from being open to the advice given about her own work, she was quick to pick up points made to other students in the workshop; all of such points—again as stressed at the beginning of this piece—as applicable to the craft of writing for children as to any other form of the writer's craft. Such as, for example, if you ever find yourself delighting in having written the kind of lyrical prose known in the trade as "a purple patch," put it away for six weeks—or better still, six months—and then reread it, as it were, "from cold."

That's when you'll find, instead, that its only effect will be to hold up your story; and from this will perhaps also learn the lesson that *every word* you write must move that story forward. It's with this lesson behind you, too, that you will inevitably have learned also the need to revise, revise, *revise*; and further, that you must always be your own most severe critic. Lest there should be any doubt, however, either on this last or on any other of the aspects of writing mentioned, let the summation at this point come now, not from me, but from one of the most respected writers of all time.

On language, it was Alexander Pushkin's published opinion that "precision and brevity are the first virtues of prose." On all else that has been discussed here, his further opinion was that "creative prose demands thought, and thought, and thought. Without thought, the most brilliant style is useless." And Pushkin, remember, included in his gifts a noted ability to write for children.

If you are right, then, in thinking that you too could do so, you may congratulate yourself on being in the best of company.

THE
THIRD EYE

THE TITLE ABOVE* is also the title of one of my twenty-five books for young readers; in this case, those who are categorized as "young adults." Its theme is perception—in effect, what the dictionary defines as "taking in with the mind and the senses." Hence the choice of its title in a phrase equating with that "eye of enlightenment" which, in some Eastern philosophies, refers to the phenomenon of the mind's ability to grasp the significance behind the outward appearance of the passing moment. Hence also the use of the same title for this essay, since it is by telling something of how the book developed that I hope eventually to make some points about perception as this relates to the literary

*Mollie Hunter, *The Third Eye*, New York: Harper & Row, 1979.

43

experience in childhood.

To indicate briefly, then, the practical basis of this development, the setting is a typical Scots Lowland village of the 1930's—the time and setting of my own childhood. The plot is woven around the lives of three sisters growing towards maturity in that setting, and the way in which their lives have intertwined with the facts behind the death of one man known to them all.

The facts in question, however, have roots that go far back into the past of all the adults concerned in the story. Also, the death has been a violent one; and under Scots law, this latter circumstance means that all the features which may have any bearing on it must be investigated by the chief law officer of the county—the Procurator Fiscal. Called for examination, therefore, is the last person to see and speak to the man before his death. This is the girl Jinty Morrison, the youngest of the three sisters; and right from the book's opening it is clear to the reader that Jinty is not only afraid of the questioning she must face, but also that she fears it because she has something to hide. A mystery is thus implied, and the rest of the book is devoted to solving that mystery.

The technique employed for this was that of extended flashback occurring while Jinty waits for her interview with the Fiscal; and the importance of that particular choice of technique will eventually emerge. But for the time being, it is the motivation for the story that must be explored, because this also has roots that go far back into the past—my own past, which holds an obsession that has persisted with me ever since early childhood.

The obsession was, and still is, with courage; the kind of courage that can nerve a person to die for an idea. I read much of this as a child, perhaps because my home had so many books (mainly of a religious nature) centering around this theme; and very often the sight that haunted me behind eyelids closed desperately tight in the attempt to lose myself in sleep was the figure of Joan of Arc or that of some other martyr burning at the stake. *Could I have endured so—for an idea?* That was the question that tormented me. And knowing myself to be one of Nature's cowards, the torment lay in the fact that the answer was always a resounding *"No!"*

Came my adolescent years in World War II, and the aftermath of war when story after story came out of Europe of men and women civilians who had resisted the evil ethos that had finally been defeated there. But too late, too late for them, came that victory, because they were the ones who had been dragged off to prison or to a concentration camp, never to be heard of again. And so they must be presumed to have died there; executed, perhaps, in a prison yard in a gray dawn with nobody, not even their executioners, to know or care who they were: nobody to know or care that the body which had slumped to the concrete had been a person who had died for an idea—surely the loneliest of all deaths? And courage, courage of this kind, *should* have witnesses!

The thought was like a cry in me, its existence adding a further and infinitely more tormenting dimension to my obsession. And far from fading as other matters faded from my mind with the progression of the postwar years, the obsession remained prominently there and grew to the point where, in some form or another, it has appeared in all my writing. Yet strangely enough, it seems to me, this has never been commented on by any of the critics who have reviewed my work—although to do the critics justice, of course, this could be because the form in which the obsession has shown has always been more oblique than direct. Until, that is, I came to write *The Third Eye.*

I had by then reached the point when it seemed to me that, unless I *was* prepared to express myself openly over something that had so long haunted me, I would have failed the writing challenge implicit in such a situation. And simply because of that, I would also have failed all those for whom I had so long affected to care—all those voiceless ones, those pitiful, nameless dead of the prison yards. Yet even so, I was sadly aware, this was still a situation where willingness to accept a challenge was not enough. All that gave me was the theme of a book, leaving me still with a plot to find, a setting, characters, and a format.

I struggled over this, struggled hard; but one can no more command the creation of a particular book than one can force growth from an infertile seed. And so, with my mind persistently remaining a blank on the book I really wanted to write, I turned to occupying my time with a project I had mentally named my "village book," writing scenes and sketches drawn from the Lowland village of my childhood, characterizing the people I had known there, and half hoping as I did so that enough might emerge eventually to cohere into a book. Almost as if I were prescient, also, I wrote particularly of one person I had known in those childhood days, a man on whose family lay a very ancient doom. And the more I wrote of him the more he haunted my imagination until he had grown there to almost the proportions of a latter-day Lear.

Yet still this work was all meaningless because, of course, it had no motivation behind it. I was very conscious, indeed, that—having already used this village as the setting for an earlier book—I was doing no more than gathering up all the bits and pieces of observation and experience that earlier book had left unused; acting, in fact, like the person I am in my nonwriting life—the thrifty housewife who cobbles together the bright bits and scraps left over from some major job of sewing, and hopes to create from them "something useful." In the process, also, I was consistently being reminded of the leading character in that earlier book, which was one that had required her personality to dominate the entire story. And since I was still holding on to a rather forlorn hope that this present exercise might just eventually also become a book, I had to find a leading character who would *not* be a dominant one; who would, on the contrary, be the kind of person who stood aside observing events, someone who would be a witness. . . .

Hold on! As if a shutter had clicked in my mind, I suddenly had the connection between the kind of leading character I wanted and the form I would give to my obsession. That Lear-like figure! There was

one way in which the tragedy in his life could be re-
solved—by an act of lonely courage. And supposing
I made that girl, the one I needed for my leading
character, a witness to the *fact* of that courage. I
would have found a voice then, would I not, to cry
out *my* witness to the courage of all those other
lonely deaths?

In a rush of triumph, I followed up this realization. I achieved a name for my girl, one that was typical of her background. Other characters began to
assemble around her, and the incidents I had earlier
written of began to relate to them. Yet still the story
did not take fire as I had thought it would—not until
I had found that format of young Jinty Morrison
reliving these incidents in flashback; because then,
I realized, I was telling of events *solely through
Jinty's perception of them*—solely, in effect (as happens with that "third eye"), *in the light of the significance she sensed for them at the moment of their
happening.*

The story, in fact, not only took fire, came really
alive, with this realization. It also took on a dimension different from that originally intended for it,
because telling everything thus—through Jinty's
perceptions—meant finally that I was writing not
only about courage and witness to courage, but fur-

ther, *about the significance of witness.*

I remember sitting back at this point, putting down my pen, and thinking about what was implied in this whole business of childhood perception. I became aware then, that the experience had clarified for me a great deal of what had previously been no more than assumptions with regard to the part that perception plays in the literary experience in childhood; which brings me now to the point of sharing the conclusions derived from my thinking.

In the book *The Third Eye*, I have drawn the girl Jinty as a person of peculiarly vivid perception; and lest this be used as an argument against what follows, I hasten to maintain that to make a leading character the personification of a book's theme is an allowable and perfectly acceptable literary device. Nevertheless, this is a device I could use only because I have a strong capacity to recall the perceptions of my own childhood; and it could be said, therefore, that this personal situation had led me to overestimate the strength and incidence of perception as a general phenomenon of childhood.

On the contrary, I think it is one which is too often underestimated; and as an example of this, I give an actual experience which I have related to the plot of the story.

A minor character in this is a nine-year-old boy called Toby. He is a sickly child, and he is blind—lonely also, since he is the only offspring of a widowed father. Jinty has formed an older-sister relationship with him, very precious to Toby since she has found a way of describing colors to him so that he can "see" them. Realizing also how important to him is his sense of touch, she brings him flowers to feel, and she is about to set off to gather for him the first snowdrops of the year when she and the rest of the children in the village school are told of his death.

She picks the snowdrops, nevertheless, but is in such a state of shock that it seems to her as if a stranger had taken possession of her body and is performing the actions for her. Her way home takes her past the village churchyard, where Toby's funeral is in progress. As she lingers at the gate there, she is noticed and beckoned in, her original purpose with the snowdrops having been surmised by another character who has knowledge of the relationship between her and Toby.

In the churchyard, she does as indicated to her. She drops the flowers down onto the coffin in the open grave; and while she does so, her perceptions are making her acutely aware of the emotions surrounding her—the pathos emanating from the fact of the child's death, the bleakness of the father's grief, the inarticulate sympathy drawing together all the men around the grave.

Now it is a fact that all the circumstances of Toby's life and death, as I have described them in the book, actually occurred in the village of my childhood; and it is only for purposes of this story that I have transmuted the relationship that my three sisters and I had with him to one in which it is Jinty alone who has this relationship. It is a fact, also, that when we were told school would close for the afternoon of his funeral, we did not rush out determined to enjoy our freedom, but went to the woods instead, to gather snowdrops. From the woods, with our hands full of flowers, we went to the village churchyard. There, with the shyness of country children, we did no more than stand dumbly at the gate, until we were noticed and beckoned in; and then, obeying the gesture made to us, we dropped the flowers down onto the little boy's coffin.

Keep in mind here that we were four sisters ranging in age from nine to twelve years; and that normally, among ourselves, we were very talkative. But from first to last throughout this whole occasion there was no word spoken among us. None of us made any suggestion about going to the woods or about picking snowdrops. None of us mentioned the boy, or the fact that he was dead, or that his funeral was due to take place. None of us proposed going to the churchyard, or waiting at the gate there. Never once, either, in all the years that have passed since that occasion, has any of us ever so much as mentioned it.

And so what am I to conclude from all this? That my sisters, when it came to the pathos of that child's death, were *less* perceptive than I was? Why then, the undiscussed and combined gathering of snowdrops? And why, once we had them, did we not take them home as we usually did, instead of going with them to the churchyard—so making the only gesture that *could* be made in these circumstances, by children like ourselves?

Why also our later silence on the details of what took place in the churchyard, and of what we observed there? Funerals in the Scotland of our childhood, after all, were always attended only by men; and so this one, for us, was a unique experience that offered endless opportunity for four little gossips to chatter afterwards about the impressions gathered there. And so what did it mean, this unnatural silence? That my sisters were also less perceptive than

I was of the smell of new-turned earth, the desolation in the father's face, the silent and awkward sympathy of the men gathered with him around that so-small grave?

If I cannot justifiably say so—and I do not believe I can—then the only difference existing at that time between my sisters and myself was that none of them had been born with the writer's mind, and thus with the desire to store up and eventually communicate in some way the significance behind the outward form of all that happened then. But I *was* so born, and since the perceptions I stored up would appear to have been common to us all, I was justified also in expressing them through the fictional character of the book. All this being so, moreover, it followed naturally that readers, too, would be just as capable of sharing the perceptions of my fictional character—always providing, of course, that sufficient reader/character identification had already been achieved. And so, it is with this proviso in mind that we now approach the nub of what is involved in relating perception to the literary experience in childhood.

We are all aware, of course, of the ways in which reader identification can be achieved at the superficial level—either in terms of a character's age, or circumstances, or, failing such obvious methods, through involving the character in events that create wishful thinking on the part of the reader. But to go more deeply than this into the process, means touching in some way the mind of one's character; and for a reader who has already identified at the superficial level, this means inevitably a touch on that reader's own mind. To touch the mind of one's character at the level of perception is to reach the deepest level of all, the one in which all feeling is rooted; and thus, with the channel to this already opened to the reader, it can truly be said that one has also reached the point where total reader identification is also rooted.

Bear in mind in all this, however, the definition of perception as one's awareness of the significance behind the outward form of the passing moment, and you will be reminded also that any real-life experience of it is therefore a very fleeting one, vanishing almost before it can be grasped. Perception, also, is a phenomenon unrelated to intelligence, or to age—except that, in the case of the latter, the very novelty of its occurrence in childhood can make this the time when its impact is most vivid. And so here, in this exception, we have a paradox, in that childhood is all too often the time when there is neither a point of reference to which one can relate the phenomenon, nor the vocabulary to express one's reaction to it.

How to resolve that paradox, then, becomes the task of the children's writer who would touch the reader at that deepest of all levels; and all my experience in this regard has taught me that this is best done by keeping in mind an equation that can be expressed thus: *Perception plus Experience plus Understanding equals Insight.*

To define how the equation is built up, I would say first that, from the very moment of birth, we are all capable of some degree of perception. To this, as we grow, is added a greater or lesser amount of experience in various of life's aspects. Further growth gives us some understanding of our experience, including that part which involves perception. And when full adulthood is reached, the achievement of perspective on the cumulative effect all this has had on us is expressed in the quality we call "insight."

To operate in the terms indicated, therefore, it is not enough to be writing simply from understanding of experience or recollection of perception, since all that would imply would be *hindsight*; and the cardinal error resulting from this, of course, is that of "writing down" to children. To write from insight, on the other hand, must always be the writer's task, whatever the type of fiction being created. Where this is for children, however, there must be a direct line of communication between insight and perception—in effect, that line which is best established by holding the whole balance of the equation consistently in mind.

Communication, however, is like blood, in the sense that it must flow at the impetus of a pumping heart, or else congeal; and if story is to be the medium of communication with children, the impetus of the writer's imagination has to be strongly behind it. Strong, too, must be that grasp on technique that enables the writer to structure a story. *But*, beyond all these things, it seems to me now and always has seemed that one must also have a willingness to think deeply about one's own humanity, both on its own account and as it concerns the generality of humankind.

This, I hold, is the only way in which one can truly enable children to open the door of literary experience; the only way one can lead them, from that first opening, through all those other doors beyond which they have not yet had the chance to explore. In the case of the book on which I have based my argument, the first of these doors was marked *Courage*. From this, to keep faith with the children for whom I wrote the book, I followed the line that ran directly from my adult insight to the perceptions of my own childhood. On the way to these, I reached the door marked *Witness to Courage*. And once this was opened for my readers, I felt that I had not only done some kind of justice to the concepts I had worked out for them, but had kept faith at last also with my brave and voiceless ones, my nameless dead.

The final door in the book was marked *Perception*; and in *all* experience of literature, for children as much as for adults, for the writer as much as for the reader, there is no greater pleasure than to open this door—and so to discover that the most significant of all the things one ever wanted to express are the very ones that lie behind it.

A
NEED
FOR HEROES

THERE IS A NEED for heroes in children's literature. This is one of my most strongly held convictions; but to assert it is far from stating what could be presumed as obvious. On the contrary, I see a need to argue its proof—first, by broadening the dictionary's definition of "hero" as "a man of courage," and second, by querying those adversary situations most commonly offered to children as encompassing the heroic ideal.

The "man of courage" implies no more than the leader type that reaches its apotheosis in Superman, sweeping down from the skies. The adversary situation is all too often presented via the standard cops-and-robbers story that shows each side as amoral as

the other, and that distinguishes the brutality of the
goodies from that of the baddies only by including
in the goodies' dialogue an occasional mealy-
mouthed platitude about saving the world for civi-
lization.

To the objective adult eye, of course, Superman is
patently a load of old rubbish; and there is no particular harm in children's reading rubbish as long as
they have plenty of good stuff available for comparison. But it has to be recognized that this presenta-
tion of the hero could also be pernicious rubbish
in that its equation of might with right elevates the
use of force to a prime ethos. As for the cops-and-
robbers theme—this is undoubtedly pernicious rubbish, and not only because it propounds the same
false ethic as Superman. Simply because there is no
difference between the tactics used by the opposing
sides, there is also a blurring of the demarcation line
in the very situation the theme ostensibly tries to
project—the struggle between good and evil. Even
more important, the same blurring process divorces
that struggle from its true battleground—the human
psyche.

Before enlarging these points, however, I should
make it clear that there is no special pleading of a religious or sectarian nature concealed in my argu-

ment, but that I speak of good and evil solely in metaphysical terms. I see in each a force that is apparently integral to human nature, yet each is antagonistic to the other—the good achieving a result that ennobles, the evil an effect that degrades. The resulting phenomenon of the human psyche perpetually at war with itself has been a fascinating one for as long as there have been thinking people; and I simply happen to be among the many on whom this fascination continues to have its effect.

To this fact, nevertheless, must be added that I am a writer, and that the mental yeast of my fascination is constantly working away beneath my surface intent to do no more than tell an entertaining tale—the result of the fermentation process being that each of my entertainments becomes also a tale of conflict, from the resolution of which emerges my personal concept of a hero. Thus, it seems to me, I cannot define that concept, nor can I show why there is a need for it in children's literature, except by illustrating from such tales; and I lead off therefore with a genre that has always been dear to my heart—that of fantasy.

It is in fantasy, I have found, that I can best marshal the opposing forces of the good-versus-evil struggle in a way that may most intrigue the younger reader; the particular advantage here being that supernaturals of the kind long held to have powers inimical to human welfare may be involved in the action, and that the threat posed by such "bad magic" can therefore be regarded as symbolic of evil. This, indeed, is precisely the situation in my native Celtic culture, in the aspect of its folklore that shows the supernaturals of its "Otherworld" as beings it can be dangerous to encounter because of these very powers; and it is from this traditional source that I have created my fantasies.*

In *The Haunted Mountain*, for example, I tell the tale of a young farmer in the Scottish Highlands, a man called McAllister who stubbornly refuses to subscribe to an ancient superstition that will deny him the use of a small part of his land. As a result, he falls foul of the supernaturals known in the Gaelic of the Highlands as the *daoine sidhe*—the "people of peace"—this name being a placatory euphemism for the creatures which retellings of folktales present in a whimsically degenerate way as fairies, but which earlier times knew and feared as the beautiful and terrible ones of the hollow hills, the powerful and revengeful magicians of the Otherworld.

The *sidhe* take revenge on McAllister by carrying him secretly to the summit of the mountain called

---

*See the chapter "Writing from a Minority Culture," and further references given there.

Ben MaDui, where he is to slave in chains for them for seven years, after which he will become a sacrifice to their own dark gods. He is presumed dead by all except his wife, Peigi Ann, who is sadly aware of his true fate. When their son, Fergus, reaches the age of twelve and also learns the truth about his father, no persuasion from his mother will deter him from setting out to the rescue; and there is nothing Peigi Ann can do then except follow a tradition common to many Highland stories of a young person setting out on a dangerous journey—the journey itself being symbolic of the journey through life. She bakes a bannock—an oaten cake. Breaking this into two unequal pieces, she offers these to Fergus along with the question:

> Will you have the big half with my curse, or the little half with my blessing?

The question also is symbolic. Will the young person set out in life taking with him all the love that has nurtured him up to that point, or will greed blind him to the one thing of value his mother can offer? A boy of twelve can become very hungry, and although he will be long away from home, Fergus is not permitted to know the significance of his mother's question; yet instinct still leads him to choose wisely. Many difficult and dangerous hours later, he reaches the place where his father is held prisoner, and then it is McAllister's turn to be afraid for the boy.

There is only one moment when rescue will be possible and only one way it can be achieved; but that way will subject Fergus to the extreme of pain, the extreme of terror. McAllister argues as Peigi Ann has done, but Fergus has inherited his father's stubborn nature. Reluctantly, McAllister gives in—but not before he realizes what answer the boy has made to that parting question from Peigi Ann, and not before he has prepared Fergus for what lies ahead.

The crucial moment arrives. Fergus takes a firm grip of his father's hand, as McAllister has warned him he must. They hear and feel the invisible coming of the *sidhe*; and then it starts—the torment, the torture to make Fergus let go of his father's hand, the testing to the ultimate of the boy's courage. Yet throughout the entire ordeal, Fergus holds on. Fergus proves that there *is* no limit to his courage. And the reason he can do so is that he has the one protection against which all the power of the *sidhe* must finally fail—one strength that must, in the end, defeat all their magic.

The logic behind all this is very simple. The whole

of magic rests on the principle that only things which are like one another can affect one another. Therefore, the one thing the *sidhe* cannot conquer is the power of human love. *They* cannot love, because they are soulless creatures. What their nature cannot encompass, they cannot understand; therefore, they cannot bring a like force to bear on it. And so, because Fergus has with him his mother's blessing, his mother's love, it is he who must finally be the victor in the conflict.

There is much further incident in the story. I have been brief, both in my approach to the incident described and in the telling of it; yet I think my account has been sufficient to show its significance as a testing moment. This same kind of moment, moreover, occurs in all my fantasies. In all of them there is conflict leading to confrontation between humans and supernaturals. In all of them it is the power of human love that achieves a final defeat of these symbolic forces of evil.

The pattern is an ancient one. It portrays a need so basic that it can be traced back to the very beginning of story—the need for reassurance against the powers of darkness, the very need underlying the belief that only steadfast love can and will prevail against those powers. If, then, this need has been so consistent, and if the belief it has bred has been essential to so many generations past, how can it possibly be denied that a similar situation exists in the minds of the present generation?

Responding to that situation, however, calls for a tale that moves on two levels. There must be a surface one of incident engrossing enough to make the reader keep on turning the pages; but the incident must be conveyed through a form of writing that enables the story to operate also on the much deeper level of symbolism. This is what I have always tried to achieve in fantasy—in effect, to entertain my readers at the same time as I express a vital element of my own philosophy. And always, to create the essential meeting point of my own and the reader's mind, I have shown the heroic action being carried by a character with whom these readers could identify—an ordinary person drawing on some emotion common to all human nature, yet still one that enables my character to transcend ordinariness, and thus to become that inspired and inspiring figure, a hero.

Only one realization is therefore required to put this concept of the hero into the context of my opening assertion about the falsity of heroes as commonly presented. It is not only adults who see Superman as superficial. *Children also do so.* Even the youngest of them—as I observe from the attitudes of my own grandchildren—realize that this figure is not real; and that when the story ends, it will be just another puppet to be put away in its box.

The situation will be different, however, with the story that has released the imagination at the same time as it has allowed the child to identify with the ordinary person as hero. The feelings evoked in the process will keep this kind of hero alive in the reader's mind; and thus, come the dark moments when no wishful concept of instant power can smother the child's knowledge of his or her own vulnerability, it is this kind of hero who may also satisfy what would otherwise be a neglected essential of childhood.

I am talking of the right to dream.

This century has been one of charters for human rights, but the right to dream has never yet been written into any charter. To the child who is granted this concept of hero, however, will be granted also at last the chance to dream himself or herself into the hero situation, literally to feel the emotion that creates the inspired and inspiring moment rising from within his or her own ordinary nature. And from the elation of that moment will also come at last an assurance of the right to compose his or her own charter.

As it is in the fantasies, so it is in my historical novels. To tell a good story is always my first intent. The development of the story stems from thoughts at a deeper level, and it always contains elements of conflicting good and evil. These books, however, are for older readers and call for a more sophisticated plot structure and narrative style. Characterization must also be more complex, and it is through characterization in the historical novels that I can best show where the true ground of the conflict lies.

To illustrate here from my novel *The Ghosts of Glencoe*, this was written around the occurrence of a truly appalling event in seventeenth-century Scotland—the Massacre of Glencoe.* The motivation for this was both personal and political. The planning was meticulous. A company of soldiers was quartered on the small Highland clan known as the Macdonalds of Glencoe. Their ostensible purpose was to collect taxes in the area of Glencoe. Their commander's secret order was that, at a given hour, his company should kill in cold blood every man, woman, and child of the Macdonald clan.

A large number of the Macdonalds escaped the intended massacre; but the weaker ones among them—the old, the pregnant women, the tiny chil-

*Mollie Hunter, *The Ghosts of Glencoe*, New York: Funk & Wagnalls, 1966.

dren—perished in the winter blizzard sweeping that night through the mountain pass that was their only way of leaving the glen. The escape, such as it was, became possible only because someone had warned them of their impending doom. That someone, according to tradition in Glencoe, was a young man called Robert Stewart; and since I have good historical warrant for the presumption that young Stewart could have been a junior officer in the company of soldiers involved, it was through him that I told the story.

I pictured Stewart in this as being the usual age for an ensign—around sixteen years—and extremely ambitious to succeed in what he perceives to be an honorable career. Like the other members of his company, he lives in amity with the Macdonalds for ten days before the order for massacre is secretly delivered to his commander only a few hours before it is due to be carried out. Stewart is stunned by the degree of treachery implicit in the order, and horrified at the idea of murdering helpless people of all ages.

It is pointed out to him that the order has come from higher up in the chain of command, and—since it is his sworn duty to obey orders from his superiors—that no one could therefore blame him for obeying this one. He is very forcibly told, also, that refusal to obey will certainly make him the first to die. The alternative of deserting his company and fleeing from the glen offers only a minimal chance of survival. Stewart is well aware, too, that the mere fact of his trying to desert will mean the end of all his career ambitions; besides which, he has been brought up in the traditions of honor, as well as those of duty. And so it is that the story—the true story of the Massacre of Glencoe—becomes also the story of his battle of conscience as he tries to decide between the man-made law, which states that he must carry out a series of atrocious murders, and the dictates of honor, which inform him of the higher law he must follow.

This is not a dilemma characteristic of any single period of history, but one that recurs in every generation. For those in my generation who failed to subscribe to that higher law, the result was the war crimes trials at Nuremberg, with all those indicted offering the same excuses that Robert Stewart could have made: "The order came from higher up"; "I had to obey or I would have been shot"; "I had no choice."

But they *did* have a choice. They could have laid career and life on the line, as young Stewart did when

he eventually decided not only to warn the Macdonalds but also to help in their escape. The guilty men
could instead have become heroes transcending their
own natures, their ordinary human nature, just as
Stewart did and from the same source of strength
that the boy Fergus drew on—because the human
emotion I have called love is really a composite of
many emotions.

Compassion plays a part in it. So does tenderness,
the impulse to self-sacrifice, and the sense that one
must follow an ideal. Where all these exist, we naturally also find such concepts as conscience, honor,
and chivalry, all of which call for absolute standards
of behavior. And where we wish to preserve such ab-
solutes, we need heroes to portray them.

But we live in times which are inimical to heroes,
times which have reached a nadir in the reductionist
thinking that postulates human nature as being no
greater than the sum of its parts. I can think of no
ground more sterile to the growth of the human
spirit, no theory more likely to debilitate the force of
creative imagination. Further, it seems to me, the
young adult novel is the form of writing most likely
to suffer fallout, as it were, from the way this has so
far affected writing in general; and since any notice I
have had as a writer for young people includes my

young adult books, it would seem only fair to question whether my theories apply to them too.

The book that most obviously meets the test, in my view, is one discussed in another connection in these pages—"The Third Eye."* The plot, as indicated there, is in the mystery surrounding the death of one man whose life has been intertwined with that of all the story's other characters. The key to the mystery lies in the fact that the man dies deliberately—as an act of self-sacrifice. He dies, in effect, for some concept greater than himself. He dies a hero.

In the unraveling of this mystery, however, my exploration of the hero concept has been more profound than in either my fantasies or my historical novels. *The Third Eye* examines the life of a whole community, ranging over past and present to gather up incidents that fit together eventually as the pieces of a mosaic fit to make a significant whole; and it is against the complete background picture thus created that the story's climax is projected.

The characters involved in the incidents are torn by conflicting emotions—sometimes noble, sometimes base. The drama played out against the book's background is dictated by the decisions arising from the conflicts, and none of the decisions is easy to

See "The Third Eye," p. 43.

make. Hardest of all is the one that has to be made by the man who chooses death, because he does not *know* that his choice will have the effect intended. He has only the hope of it to give him the courage for his act of self-sacrifice—the hope of one positive, heroic gesture overriding all the destructive possibilities implicit in the negative course of his refraining from the act.

The opposite of hero is coward; and as cowardice is often disguised as a negative quality, so evil is often similarly disguised. To compromise in recognition of this fact is simply to blur even further the essential line of demarcation. To show someone daring to take positive action in the hope of good, when the safe alternative of nonaction gives acquiescence to potential harm, is the ultimate step in that recognition—and, therefore, also is the final possible step in the creation of a hero. The fact that our times are inimical to heroes does not alter the truth of this; and such verities must somehow be conveyed to those youngsters so hopefully referred to as the young adults of our world.

I began this argument by quoting the broad dictionary definition of "hero" as "a man of courage" and went on to refine this in my own terms. Yet I find I must ultimately return to the dictionary for

the most penetrating of all the possible definitions—
the hero is one who has "greatness of soul."

The phrase is archaic. It would appear to have become obsolete so far as literature in general is concerned. But in children's literature, at least, there is
still scope for heroes distinguished by this quality,
still a function for heroes to fulfill, and—blessedly
for the hope of the world—it would seem that the
young readers themselves still feel a need to encounter them.

IF
YOU
CAN READ

"IF YOU CAN READ, you can educate your-self." On the occasion I coined this statement for the benefit of a group of children's librarians, some of them were so struck by its implications that they asked me to inscribe it in their individual copies of my own work for young readers; and I did so with a sense of great awareness of the personal connotations it held.

"What influences have there been on you as a writer?" This is a type of question frequently posed to those of my profession and, in my case, frequently avoided; but here and now, at least, is one occasion where it requires answering to the extent of claiming a reading childhood as a strong and primary influence. Another was the pattern of my schooling—a traditional one, this, with grammatical analysis, précis writing, and sentence construction accepted as an essential part of English lessons. Family circumstances, however, abruptly put paid to schooling when I was still only fourteen years old. Earning, rather than learning, became overnight my portion; yet I still had a great ragbag of questions to which I desperately wanted answers, and I was determined to be a writer.

I left school thinking that my only equipment for this aim was a fluency in reading and a great love of words; but although I did not then recognize it as such, I also had a writer's ear for the fall of language, and to guide my first efforts, I had that solid grounding in grammar.

Again, however, I did not recognize the good fortune of such a grounding, nor could I then guess at its essential nature. My only clear feeling was that I might be able secretly to plunder the stores of knowledge otherwise denied me; and so, at the first moment possible, I trailed my ragbag of questions into the most august library I could find. There I took out my biggest question—the one clearly labeled "GOD"—sat down, and began to read.

Very soon, then, I discovered that God has many

faces, and from the thickets of comparative religion I began to disentangle the stems making up the pattern of Celtic folklore. I also began to see that a people's folklore is only one face of a coin, of which the other face is that people's written history. I became aware of reflections in both sides of this particular coin—reflections of many things about my own village that had puzzled me before that time and which still intrigued me.

It is commuter country now, that part of Lowland Scotland which holds the village of my childhood. Tarmac roads lie like a tangle of black spaghetti where once the gold of barley harvest was heavy. The rich red earth plowed by great teams of shining Clydesdales is sick with spreading bungalow rash; but in those days our village was only a small place— little more than a farm with cottages grouped around it and a single street of cottages running past the farm.

Whitewashed, and roofed with the mellow red of ogee pantiles, these cottages crouched small in gardens spilling over with wallflowers and hollyhocks, stocks, peonies, and dahlias rioting out of the fertile Lowland earth. The bee hum that lingered over the flowers' profusion had been disturbed by nothing more than the voice of the martyred George Wishart preaching the Reformation. The village street had seen no more exciting occasion than a contentious little man called John Knox arrogantly preceding the gentle presence of Wishart with the unwanted symbol of a sword borne aloft. The Dene—the lane running from the village to the cold waters of the Firth of Forth—had witnessed no darker sight than a coven of sixteenth-century witches who had "convened at the Dene fute, and daunced thir."

The village was remarkable only in having remained unremarkable through all the centuries of turbulent history which had washed over that corner of southeast Scotland. Yet history was there in it, the people's history written small in small recurrent events and persistent customs, which only the wondering eye of a child would find worth more than a glance.

The "flittings"—the removals when farm laborers exchanged a job in one parish for a job in another— why were they so frequent? Knowing nothing of the complicated agrarian pattern that had produced these landless peasants, I watched them loading carts with their possessions, piling straw on top, then loading their children onto the straw. The dangling boots of the children were tackety-soled and— bought for growth—grotesquely big for their thin legs. The dusty gold of the straw could not conceal how scuffed the furnishings were; and as the carts trundled away, I recognized uneasily that there went people even poorer than my poverty-stricken family.

At the farm, too, when I gathered with the other children for the "poor-oot"* [the coins that were always thrown after a wedding] I wondered at the cruelty of the bride's reception. Why did they not throw confetti or rice over her as she ran up the path to the house? Why did they pelt her with stones until she screamed and cried and swore at them, her face all red and ugly above the white dress? The bride reached the door. The hostile stone throwers became cheerful guests throwing the expected coins to the waiting children. The bride was taken in triumph into the house, and I was acutely aware of a ritual of some kind having been enacted.

The history of the village was there, too, in the speech of its people—the Doric, which I also spoke then as fluently as the standard English required from me at school. Experience and reading began to come closer together. The reflections became clearer. I had not known before that Doric was anything except a peasant tongue—a dialect spoken only in such rural areas as my birthplace. Yet here was I discovering from books that until the beginning of the eigh-

*English form—"pour-out"

teenth century, Doric had been a language in its own right, the language of the country's law and church as well as that of everyday speech in the Lowlands; the language of kings, courtiers, and gentlefolk as well as that of the common people; the language of the greatest among the *makars*—the poets of Scotland.

Here I was, in fact, taking the first steps to explore the two great interests of my life—the history and folklore which were later to provide the source material for the greater part of my writing—and beginning to prove, in this process, the truth of the dictum I was later to state in very different circumstances: "If you can read, you can educate yourself." There was something I used often to be told as a child, however—a piece of homespun wisdom which was intended to teach me the potential of the conditional tense, and which ran, "*If* is a little word with a very big meaning."

In this present context, then, "if you can read" must be taken to have cautionary as well as hopeful connotations. No obstacles except those of family circumstances were encountered on my personal road to literacy, but basic methods of schooling have changed from the traditional, book-oriented pattern that was mine. Guidance now comes, to some extent, through the study of linguistics, and there is one theory current in this study which might well place some sort of obstacle in the modern child's road to the same goal. The account of my own experience, therefore, has been needed as a preliminary to arguing against this theory; and my first term of reference for that argument is a definition of everything implied in the word "language."

In its broadest sense, the word simply means "human speech." More precisely, it would be defined as a variety of speech or a body of words and idioms, especially that of a nation. To take in all the nuances of meaning in the word, however, one would have to say that language is the expression and communication of emotions and ideas between human beings by means of speech and hearing, the sounds spoken and heard being systemized and confirmed by usage among a given people over a period of time.

The word "dialect" is my second term of reference, and here it should be noted that dictionary definitions do not agree except in declaring dialect to be a variety or form of language peculiar to a district, class, or trade. This, one dictionary may say, means that dialect is distinguished from the standard or literary form of a language. Another dictionary may maintain that dialect is not necessarily other than standard or literary form; and this second opinion, in my view, is the more correct of the two.

To give the example closest to my heart, I refer back to that Doric speech of my childhood. This, like the speech that was common to England and the Lowlands of Scotland until the fifteenth century, is based on Anglo-Saxon; but, whereas English speech from that time evolved into the form in which we have it today, Scottish Lowland speech continued to receive into itself influences from German, French, Dutch, Norse, Danish—from all those languages, in fact, which permeated it through military or commercial contact with the eastern seaboard of Scotland. A most flexible language form which proved capable of the highest literary expression was the result, and it was only the shift of political power brought about by the Union of Scottish and English Parliaments which reduced it from the status of a main-stem language to that of a dialect.

Even though one tries to be precise in all these definitions, then, it can be seen that there is still a wide diffusion of ideas involved and that we are now in a complex area of debate. There was scant acknowledgment of this, however, in a lecture which first brought the disputed theory to my attention and in which "language" and "dialect" were also the terms of reference. "Dialect" was given the very limited definition of "any form of speech mutually acceptable within a group or area." On the question of language, the definition took the form of the query, "What is standard English?" And this was answered by saying that it was "just the way educated people had agreed to speak." In effect, therefore—and again in the lecturer's own words—it was "just a dialect of English"; and, as such, it was no more to be considered correct speech than any other dialect of the same language. If everyone in a social group, for instance, were to have mutual understanding that "I don't want no water" meant "I don't want any water" (the example actually used), condemnation of the double negative would have no grammatical validity but would simply show social prejudice against it.

An experiment in speech-pattern testing was quoted in this connection, its finding being that there was high-frequency use of the double and multiple negative at the lowest end of the social scale, and vice versa. The automatic reaction to this find, it was claimed, was to correlate class with degrees of so-called correctness in speech—thus proving social prejudice as the governing factor in deciding the comparative acceptability of the speech patterns tested.

Correlation of class with educational opportunity was not mentioned, although this would seem also to be part of any relevant conclusion. The lecturer continued, instead, with making his main point—that no form of dialect was either more or less significant in cultural terms than the dialect referred to as standard English, and that this cultural equation should be extended to include, as a dialect, any form of ungrammatical speech which is the product of group inclination.

Relating all this to the classroom situation, then, it was stressed that group inclination was precisely the factor making such a dialect a viable means of communication among those deploying it. Thus, it would serve only to confuse and disorient if a child were expected to speak only standard English in school while, in other situations, speaking in the ungrammatical way acceptable to his group. And, so far as reading was concerned, that child would automatically set up the mental process of translation required of any dialect speaker confronted with a written form of standard English.

The logic deployed in reaching this conclusion may not have been impeccable—in an hour's lecture, after all, one cannot cover every point arising from a subject; but there is still so much of sound reason in the conclusion itself that its ultimate flaw is not readily apparent. The whole reading experience of the child, however, and ultimately through that, the reading experience of the adult, could be affected by this flaw. And so, as the first step in making it apparent, I find it useful to take a further look at the word "dialect"—also from the viewpoint of the classroom situation.

The main-stem language that historical circumstance has relegated to the lower status of a dialect would seem to be the prime form to consider in any such examination; and the Doric—the Lowland Scots which was my natural speech in childhood—provides me with a good example. As I have previously mentioned, Doric has the scope and flexibility which make it rank high as a literary medium; and had it continued to be officially the language of Lowland Scotland in my day, I would still have been taught in a tongue that would have enabled me to be a writer. To reach more than a minority of English-language readers, however, I would either have had to depend on translation or else have had to learn English as a second language showing differences in syntax from that of the Doric.

"*Gae ye doon thon wey,*" for instance, would have had to be rendered as "Go down that way."

"*Gie's ower tae me thon ashet*" would have had to be "Let me have that plate." These differences are slight, however, and the common root of English and Doric means that much of the apparent variance of vocabulary is only a matter of differing pronunciation. It could be feasible, therefore, to teach the two side by side, with either one as the officially approved language; and I am far from alone in thinking that the lack of any attempt to do this has meant a cultural loss for many generations of Scots.

Much the same argument could be applied to those English dialects which have regional scope and which—through this very fact—have preserved many usages enriching to the language as a whole. Similar value exists in those dialects spoken in communities supported by a way of life, such as fishing or farming, which relates primarily to the rhythms of earth and where there are skills to be communicated directly from one generation to another. And—although to a much lesser extent—any dialect peculiar to a trade or craft confers this same value.

This, to me, is the true value of dialect in the classroom—as an aid to the teaching of language generally and as an aspect of speech to be seized on for its enriching contribution to the standard form of a language, with every child who is unselfconscious in the use of dialect encouraged to evaluate it in relation to the standard form; and, by thus learning to place words in the appropriate context of either dialect or standard forms of speech, to be made ultimately more aware of the definitive values of these words. The lecturer quoted must certainly also have intended his views to be an aid towards this highly desirable end. One cannot conceive otherwise; and so, in being definitive in argument from my side, I may possibly have cleared the ground for consideration of that dialect which may be termed so only because of its lack of any acknowledged grammatical form.

A prime point to note here is that small children extend their usages of speech as unselfconsciously as they acquire language itself. An infant playing with a toy car learns "car" by repetition of the word, indicates ownership of the toy by a gesture, and later emphasizes the gesture by stating "my car" or "mine car." "Mine" or "my" may persist through the infant years, but as speech extends to cover more complicated circumstances, the usage is gradually settled as my. In the first school years there is a similar settling-in period for all children beginning to use language as the prime medium of learning. On an average basis, varying degrees of ungrammatical speech is the normal pattern in a class of infants, whatever the social background of the individual child; and it is only the sifting process of learning through language which gradually reveals to them that the teacher's way of speaking is the educated adult norm.

This is the stage where a child with one speech pattern at home and another in school may quickly become disadvantaged. Too frequent correction, or correction which makes him in any way ashamed of his grammatical errors, will only make him tongue-tied in school and all the more vocally assertive of social loyalties outside of school. A block to learning will have been established—one that can only become greater over the years—a situation well known to skilful teachers but one which they have ways of avoiding. I quote one long practiced by a clever teacher of my acquaintance.

To use "went" and "gone" correctly can present difficulties to children, and when the school bell rings, a child may obligingly inform this lady, "Mrs. Sharp, the bell has just went." The pattern then is first to thank the child for the reminder and then to explain *to the whole class* why the correct word to use would have been "gone." The next time the bell rings, the teacher herself will draw attention to it with the announcement, "Children, the bell has just went." Immediately then, she will mime great dismay at her own "mistake," while the class—delighted to be able to correct her—will chorus, "*Gone!* Mrs. Sharp. The bell has just *gone!*"

There is sound psychology at work here. A correct grammatical use has been established, not by admonition but by bolstering the children's confidence in themselves. But all this still begs the question of *why* children should be guided towards correct or standard use of their language; and at the heart of this question lies the statement that an ungrammatical form of language has cultural validity equal to that of the established grammatical form. To expose the flaw in this statement, therefore, one must look beyond the spoken to the written word and dismiss, first of all, the defense that a process of translation will bridge all differences.

There is a flavor of elitism in this—that same elitism which refers to standard English as a "dialect" mutually acceptable among educated people; and this defense, in my view, places its subject as nothing more than a stranger in a land with a language he has only imperfectly grasped but which—since his stay is to be temporary, in any case—he need not master in its entirety.

By far the more justifiable approach, surely,

would be the one which recognizes the standard or literary form of a language as a phenomenon to be exploited in the service of all the heritors of those who have evolved it, the aim of such an approach being to use an agreed-upon syntax as the basis of practical understanding for all; and, in the cultural field, to permit this syntax to yield experiences which, again, may be enjoyed in common. Surely, also, there is no one who would dispute this aim—and here the nub of the argument is reached. There is a condition attached to attaining it, one that I can best describe by reverting to my earlier mention of the writer's ear for the fall of language.

This latter is a gift, an endowment innate to the individual mind. And yet—strangely enough, it might seem—the sensitivities of this natural appreciation are never offended by the standard form of a language. They are gratified, rather, by its apparent ability to verbalize subtleties of thought, and from the sound created, to cull sure harmony and inevitable rhythm; and this, on consideration, is far from strange, after all. The successive peaks of development in a language are reached through its literature, and so it could fairly be said that the shape and ultimate confirmation of its syntax have been tested by the ear of many writers through many generations.

Such gifts as the writer may have, however, are only the basis of his art. The technique to deploy these gifts must be acquired, the discipline to apply technique learned; and—reverting again to my own experience—I would not have been able even to begin research into my material unless I had been able to read fluently and with immediate comprehension. Without my solid base of grammatical skills, I would not have been able to achieve even the slightest grasp of the writer's technique.

Years of persistent effort lay ahead for me in this work, of course; but even so, it had still taken an effort on my part simply to reach that childish starting point—and this is the condition that attaches to the sharing of the potential of any language. As it is with the writer in his effort to exploit that potential, so it must be with the reader in his effort to grasp the syntax from which the potential will flower.

The creativeness of the writer is expressed in attempting to communicate through language deployed to its most striking advantage; and thus the enjoyment of the experience he offers to share is lifted to a level beyond the expression of the non-creative mind. But if the reader has not made his own effort towards a grasp of syntax, the effect of this heightened enjoyment will be lost; the experience itself will pass him by.

On the other hand, if the reader's grasp of syntax is sufficient to let him understand and appreciate that of the writer, his perception of the experience will be all the sharper; his enjoyment of it will also take place at that same high level. And this, of course, is the whole reward of reading: to have one's imagination carried soaring on the wings of another's imagination; to be made more aware of the possibilities of one's mind through the workings of another mind; to be thrilled, amazed, amused, awed, enchanted in worlds unknown until discovered through the medium of language, and to find in those worlds one's own petty horizons growing ever wider, ever higher.

Where does all this leave the child who is not directly encouraged to differentiate between grammatical and ungrammatical patterns of speech, whose vocabulary will remain limited as a result of the syntactical limitations of the latter, and who, in his school years, will constantly have to rely on translations to link the two? With the reading difficulties stemming from the efforts to make such links, what incentive will there be for him to continue reading once the school years are over? On consideration of all such points, can it truly be said that standard

English has no higher cultural validity than the form of dialect which—in the last analysis—is only speech structured by nothing more than the mutual inclinations of the uninstructed?

To relate all these questions to the children's literature available at present is to realize all the more sharply the implications they hold, since never before in the history of the genre has there been such scope, such choice, such a generally high standard of writing. Never before, therefore, has there been so much to tempt the reader towards the establishment of basic reading skills, never before such opportunity to encourage these skills to expand; and surely it would be a retrograde step to indulge any theory that could minimize this opportunity? It must be remembered, also, that the chief reading experience of today's adult took place in the school years; and how can so unfortunate a circumstance be avoided in future generations unless its factors are isolated for recognition?

If you can read, you can educate yourself, and education is not a process of cramming in knowledge but of leading out the possibilities of the mind. Education expands the personality, as reading does. Doors open, new worlds are discovered, barriers disappear, as they do in reading. Education and reading—with hindsight on my own experience to bolster conviction, I make a categorical statement of my own theory on the relationship between the two.

As long as equality of opportunity in education remains a far-distant goal, we shall have a population divided on the social lines of a mandarin elite to which all culture is open, with a great submass distinguished by its defensive use of varying group idioms and, consequently, by minimal reading inclinations and skills. As long as this situation holds for a generation of children for whom the beauties of language are only selectively opened and who are not equally encouraged to grasp the whole structure of that language, we will have a generation which will not equally be given the incentive to read.

The alternative opportunity of self-education through reading will not therefore equally present itself; and thus, until that distant goal is reached at last, the dividing line between the educated and noneducated should be renamed as that between the reader and the nonreader.

As one whose whole life has benefited from crossing that line, I can see no excuse now for perpetuating its existence. As one who was early given the basic knowledge needed to make the crossing, I can see no defense now for any theory which considers such knowledge unimportant. On the contrary, I contend as strongly as lies within my power that an understanding of the grammar of one's own language is essential to its use in everything beyond the immediate environs of one's group—from which it follows that any teaching which does not acknowledge this fact must have the result, in the end, of confining the children concerned to the limits of their particular group.

My own childhood experience was the fortunate thing which meant I could never be so confined, and I have not spent my working life as a children's writer to the end of tolerating the possibility of a lesser fortune for young people of other generations. Not for a moment, either, will I consider it unimportant to my readers that I have a great love of language and an equal respect for the structure on which it is based. On the contrary, I believe—I passionately believe—that the disciplines of craft can and should enable me not only to hold their interest with a story but also to communicate a feeling that will imbue their minds with something of that same love and respect. Why should it be otherwise? Every child is a human being of only partly known potential, and how can that potential ever be fully discovered until it has fed on the best one has to offer?

It is an axiom that the reading child becomes the reading adult, and I have tried to argue the case for what I consider must be the ambient situation for the child who is to have any real hope of following that progression. Opinion may be against me, and if so, I can do no more than make a final declaration springing from the reaction of a teacher sitting beside me on the occasion when I heard the opposite case argued. Turning towards me with an expression that seemed to convey dismay at what she had heard with determination to resist its application, the lady exclaimed, "They're taking away the last sure ground we have to stand on!"

I will not cede one inch of that ground. To the last breath I will defend its value; and to the last, also, I will insist that every child has the right to an equal share in that value.

WRITING FROM A MINORITY CULTURE

THE VIEW from the study where all my books for children are written shows a landscape characteristic of the country from which these derive—that of my native Scotland. There's a world of difference, therefore, between this outlook and the one available to most of my readers—and that statement is not intended in its literal sense.

What concerns me, rather, is the figurative aspect to be found in the fact that I write and always have written from a minority culture. Yet I work in English, the first language of the world's largest group of literate peoples. It's true, also, that those unfamiliar with Scotland tend to think of its people as primarily British and only secondarily Scottish. And so who *are* the Scots that they should deem otherwise?

This is a large question—but I am concerned with it only as it affects the literary tradition developed within that minority culture, and specifically as this relates to writing for children. My immediate recall, therefore, is of myself as an eleven-year-old listening to my history teacher—a handsome young man who had so charmed me that I paid devout attention while he rapidly sketched the antecedents of our class— i.e., all of us being Scots, we were descended primarily from the Celts who first colonized the British Isles. And then came the pedantic joke he had been preparing for us.

The later Anglo-Saxon invasion of England, he explained, took over the whole of that country; but it was only a minority of Angles who worked their way north into Scotland. "In other words"—and again came that attractive grin that had made me so heartsick for him—"it was the obtuse Angles who went south, and the acute Angles came north."

I laughed, of course, along with the rest of the class. But I was still interested enough to sense an ironic core of truth in the joke; and that interest continued to the point where I was later to discover that those Anglians who took over the fertile southeast of Scotland—the Lowlands—and made Anglo-Saxon the language there, were most certainly a very hard-headed lot.

Cultivators primarily, their innate shrewdness meant that they had a flair for trade as well. Once they were firmly settled in Scotland, also, they became notorious for a tradition that still lasts—that of venturing far from home to make careers as soldiers of fortune, as scholars, and as exponents of the practical sciences. Their continuing links with other countries were therefore as much in the field of ideas as of commerce, and it was from the society created by them that there emerged Scotland's long-standing tradition of literacy.

The Gaelic-speaking Celts, on the other hand, walked always with pride and poetry as their twin companions. Pride came from their clan system, in which every individual could trace some connection with the Chief, who himself could claim descent from some hero of the far past; but it was this very pride of lineage, unfortunately, which made them so vainglorious and quarrelsome that they were slowly but very surely quite outmaneuvered by those very practical Lowlanders.

Poetry existed for the Gaels in the very structure of their language; and this, combined with the fact that they were a pastoral people with a purely oral culture, meant that song and story were integral features of their lives. They had a great sensitivity, also, to natural phenomena, especially those of the area that became their last stronghold—the mountainous region of the Highlands. Concomitant with this was a deep vein of mysticism that led them to treat the supernatural as simply part of the totality of life; and it is these two latter characteristics that can be traced yet in at least one aspect of the deep concern with the supernatural so often found in writing from Scotland.

Two more disparate peoples could hardly be imagined; yet they still managed anciently to form a sovereign nation that successfully fought off England's long series of attempts to conquer it. Nor did it become part of the political entity of Great Britain until, in 1707, it made a Treaty of Union with England. Long, long before that time, however, many centuries before it, Scotland had achieved its own body of law, its own form of religion, its own system of education; and all these—the three most powerful cultural influences in any country—were guaranteed to it under that treaty.

All these, also, were and still are, distinctively different from their counterparts in England. And so, finally, if one sets beside these circumstances the fact that the Scots number a mere five million among the hundreds of millions of those with English as a first language, it becomes quite evident that it is indeed a minority culture from which I write. The literary tradition developed within that culture is therefore also distinctively Scots; and this is not least in the preoccupation already mentioned—its concern with the supernatural.

There are two strains to this kind of writing, and the one influenced by life in the Lowlands has roots that tend to produce a flower of most sinister form. This is not to be wondered at, however, since the Angles who ousted the original Celtic stock in this area were of Nordic Teutonic origin, and so, in pagan times, were heirs to a predominantly dark concept of the supernatural. This latter, also, found a suitably gloomy alternative in the puritanical form of Christianity that was later to condition every aspect of their thinking; and thus, from the days of minstrelsy onwards, there has continued to be that dark streak in Scottish writing.

In ballad form, for example, this tells often of the "demon lover" of young girls—in effect, the Judeo-Christian "devil" in the form of a handsome young man. In novels, from the early nineteenth century to the present day—from James Hogg with his *The Pri-*

vate Memoirs and Confessions of a Justified Sinner, through Robert Louis Stevenson's *Dr. Jekyll and Mr. Hyde*, to much of the work of Muriel Spark—it surfaces in the same form; a fascination with duality of personality that tacitly admits to equal fascination with and fear of the omnipresence of "devilish" forces.

The purely Celtic concept of the supernatural, on the other hand, had no such macabre aspects;* and what this concept boiled down to in story terms was that, although it could be frightening to meet with Otherworld creatures such as the "kelpie"† or the "grollican,"‡ there was nothing really unusual in this. That Otherworld of Celtic belief, after all, was not some infernal region, but simply existence on a plane other than that inhabited by flesh and blood— one that allowed its creatures to be visible or invisible, just as they chose.

The outcome of any such encounter depended entirely, therefore, on its circumstances. If these spelled danger, there was always some countermagic that could be used against the magic of the Otherworld entity that had brought the danger. If the entity was friendly, it was even possible for the human to make

---

*For further elucidation see the essay "The Otherworld" in Mollie Hunter, *Talent Is Not Enough*, New York: Harper & Row, 1976.
†Mollie Hunter, *The Kelpie's Pearls*, New York: Harper & Row, 1976.
‡Mollie Hunter, *The Wicked One*, New York: Harper & Row, 1977.

some gain from the meeting. For those who were either bold enough or experienced enough, too, it was further possible to enter the Otherworld at will, and—provided one kept carefully to the rules that governed it—to enjoy its strange delights, and depart again in peace.

There is nothing in human knowledge that either confirms or denies the validity of the concept inspiring the beliefs behind such tales—any more than there is, of course, for that other and much darker concept. Of the two, however, it is still that of the Celts which is more to be preferred by any Scottish writer who shares the traditional preoccupation with the supernatural and whose work happens to be for children.

The very nature of that concept, indeed—the mere idea of magic being possible in everyday circumstances, but still also with safeguards against any of its terrors, and even the possibility of some final reward—is a natural basis of fantasy for young readers. Or so it would seem, at least. Yet even so, the tale that springs from such a basis cannot succeed in truly creating fantasy unless the writer is one who does not seek either to question or to explain, but simply—*like the storytellers of ancient times*—to convey the adventure of contact with the Otherworld, the awe that this inspires, and very often, too, the sheer poetry of the experience.

> For it is no use trying to account for things in Fairyland; and one who travels there soon learns to forget the very idea of trying to do so, and takes everything as it comes; *like a child, who, being in a chronic condition of wonder, is surprised at nothing.* [My italics]*

It was one of Scotland's most noted writers of fantasy who commented thus, and the situation since his time has not changed. The compelling power of the Otherworld exerts its influence still, but only on those naturally open to it—in effect, those who feel that power, as it were, like a current in the blood. The corresponding sense of the marvelous is still, as it always has been, a phenomenon of childhood. And the joy of the Scottish children's writer, creating fantasy for children of present times, is that this is still what makes it possible for each to find, in the other, the perfect complement.

One other and well-known preoccupation of writing in Scotland is the historical novel. So strong is this preoccupation, indeed, that the literary scene in Scotland could be said to breed historical novels to the same extent as a pond of still water breeds flies—or has done, at least, ever since the days of their great

*George MacDonald, *Phantastes*, Grand Rapids, MI: Eerdmans, 1981.

progenitor, Sir Walter Scott. It could justly be said also, nevertheless, that a fair number of his successors have brought to the genre more of enthusiasm than of skill. But even so, there have still always been enough of those more accomplished in this aspect of Scottish literary tradition to have shaped outside opinion to the view—best expressed by Peter Hollindale—that the historical novels created from it are "one of its established forms and glories."

As to why all this should be so, the reasons are various, but all of them are compelling. The country is a small one, it's true, but much of its landscape is of a grandeur that strikes dramatically on the senses. Its internal history has been colorful, extremely turbulent at times, and at times also most romantically involved with this dramatic terrain. Its population has always been small—up till the end of the eighteenth century, a mere fraction of what it is today; but even so, and against all attempts at invasion and other less open means, the tiny national entity formed by this population has succeeded over many centuries in maintaining its identity *as* a nation.

The stories bred from all this were, of course, legion; but more than that, they were also of a character that varied widely from the romantic to the rumbustious, from the tenderly moving to the tough and chilling, from the hilarious to the heroic. The sparseness of population, also, together with the passion for genealogy inherited from the Celts, meant that blood ties with those involved were easily identifiable; and where no blood tie existed, the small land mass meant that other connections were just as easily traced.

As for the figures that loomed largest out of such tales, these became legends in their own day, not only because of all the other factors already mentioned; but simply because—whether hero, heroine, rogue, or eccentric—they really were somehow larger than life. Since ancient times, also, there has been in Scotland the tradition of story in its most lasting form—that of the ballad. And so, with this finally to ensure continuity, it was inevitable that the stories in question would be passed down from generation to generation, retold again and again until they became, as it were, a sort of national treasury in which all could feel they had a share.

That feeling still persists, the result of which is that the Scots live very close to their past—so close, indeed, that they still identify strongly with its events and personalities; and it is precisely this sense of *personal* identification that has enabled Scottish writers to give to the historical novel that hard edge of reality and that urgency of communication which distinguishes it from other work in the same genre.

Always also, in the best of these, there will be a strong story line—an element which would seem to spring from another enduring characteristic of the Celtic culture. This is the sheer *love* of story which, in Scotland, shows itself in the fact that the most commonly heard of all conversational remarks is some variant or other of this phrase:

Aye, well, that reminds me of a wee story.

I recall, for example, an American friend of mine coming back from a stroll near my home in the Highlands and telling me in a somewhat dazed manner that he had encountered two men within five minutes' walking distance of one another, and that the conversation of each had been to tell him a story.

"And," he added wonderingly, "their stories were just fascinating. Yet they weren't professional story-tellers. They were just ordinary working men."

Quite true, of course. But they were also Highlanders, with a tradition of storytelling going back into prehistory. Yet even so, that experience could equally well have happened to my friend anywhere in Scotland, so strong is the current of story in every part of it, so much is there to tell, and so well loved and familiar is all that has to be told.

When it comes to rendering something of all this, then, in the form of an historical novel—and especially, as so often happens in Scotland, when such a novel is for young readers—it is a combination of all the factors mentioned which can result in it being what is effectively an *adventure* novel. That hard edge of reality and that urgency of communication are the factors enabling these readers to identify with the book's characters, and thus with the incidents in which they are involved. But most importantly—and simply because young people seldom are really interested in the past as such—it is that strong story line which can carry them along from incident to incident and, rather than making these seem like a careful restructuring of events long dead, can give to them instead the same impact as that of some true-life and exciting tale of the present day.

Important as this last feature is, however, in *all* writing for children, it is still the case—as any writer from any culture will testify—that it is not the final one needed to present even the most gripping of stories in written terms. The craftsmanship to weld all of a book's elements into a smoothly structured whole must be there also; and the circumstances here for the Scottish writer relate directly to something already mentioned—the country's long-standing tradition of literacy.

The growth of this tradition—the first of its kind in Europe—was such that it created considerable respect for all forms of the written word. That included writing for children—a branch of the craft from which there was as high a standard of craftsmanship demanded as from any other, and which was therefore valued accordingly. The assumption behind that demand, also—and this is where the tradition of literacy specifically applies—was that children are as entitled as are adults to the best of a writer's skills.

There is striking testimony to this, indeed, in some rueful words penned by Robert Louis Stevenson—this time in his role as a children's writer. "I am engaged on writing a little book for boys," he wrote in a letter to his mother, "and it is such *hard work.*" The italics are Stevenson's own, and the "little book for boys" was his classic, *Treasure Island.*

Implicit in these same demands of the native literary tradition, also, is a second assumption on writing for children—one that has its root in a highly significant aspect of the Celtic culture. This was the *ceilidh,* the social occasion that saw a group of families meeting to entertain themselves and one another with songs, and with stories. The subject matter of all these could—and did—range from fairy tales to dramatic accounts of events significant to all those present; from the fanciful, in effect, to the historical; all of which was therefore supremely important both as food for the imagination and as a means of transmitting a record of such events.

Family gatherings meant that children were naturally also included in a *ceilidh*. Occasionally, too, a tale could be told specifically for them. The assumption generally made about the children present, however, was that they could—and would—absorb from any other stories whatever appealed *intuitively* to the individuals among them.

So we have both these assumptions continuing into the literary tradition of Scotland, in that writing for children frequently crosses over that strict demarcation line found elsewhere between "children's" and "adult" literature—and by doing so, incidentally, has won readers of all ages to its side.

I do not believe, either, that there is anyone who would doubt the validity of the first of these assumptions—i.e., that children are entitled to the best a writer has to offer. But, as regards the second—and despite the comment made in defense of it—the allowance it makes for the element of intuition is not likely to be acceptable to those firmly wedded to the idea of reading carefully graded according to standards officially set for all of any particular age group. Nor am I aiming here at those who must, perforce, apply some sort of standard in educational terms, but at those others concerned with children's literature who have forgotten that—all other considerations apart—reading is for *pleasure*.

I recall keenly from own childhood a person of this same kind, and also the curt admonition that always came along with the gesture of snatching a longed-for book from my hand:

You're far too young for that!

That self-appointed guardian of my childhood reading is long dead; and I can only regret now an attitude that showed her so ignorant of her own country's traditions. As to those more enlightened ones that now prevail generally, there is all the more satisfaction in knowing that the boys and girls of today so often can, and just as often do, enhance their reading pleasures by cross-shelving between books written specifically for their age group, and those published for a presumed adult market.

It seems a matter of considerable interest too, that this practice leads every now and then to young readers taking over as "their" book one that has been published for adults and which continues to sell in that market—*The Catcher in the Rye*, for example, or *Lord of the Flies*. And so, to relate all this finally to that second assumption, it seems more than feasible that the literary tradition which gives credit to an intuitive factor at work in young minds is perfectly correct in doing so.

There is still, however, a wide area of concern for those working from within that tradition—specifically, also, if their books are set in Scotland itself (which latter, of course, is not necessarily the case), and even more specifically if those books are for children. Scotland, after all, is very largely *terra incognita* to most people outside its borders; and what applies to adults in this respect inevitably applies even more to children.

What one faces here, then, is an exacerbated form of a technical problem in the structuring of any book—that of orienting readers towards the story's location and its place in time. This is done, normally, by planting early on in the text some kind of "markers" towards these features—markers that readers will instantly recognize; but no such easy solution is open to the Scottish writer with a book in which terrain and time will almost certainly be unknown to most young readers—and that writer has accordingly to be extremely ingenious in finding ways to provide this essential orientation. *

A second area of concern affecting any book set in Scotland is that, even although one is writing in English, there is a problem in language terms—the fact of the matter here being that colloquial speech in Scotland differs considerably from the English in use elsewhere. The variation is very much wider, indeed, than that between—say—English English and American English; but whatever these differences are, they all stem from the one circumstance.

This, quite simply, is that the original Anglo-Saxon of Lowland speech developed in England through "Inglis" into "English," while in Scotland the process was of Anglo-Saxon developing into Doric—or "Scotis" as this was called until the eighteenth century gradually saw it being transformed into the standard English of today.† Many of the words of the old Scots language, however, are still in common use—so many indeed that, to those unfamiliar with Scottish colloquial speech, it can often be quite incomprehensible.

For the writer, therefore, although this presents no problem as regards narrative, it very much does raise a problem in terms of dialogue; the essence of

*See "If You Think You Can Write," p. 19.
†See "If You Can Read," pp. 79 and 82.

which problem being that one must avoid checks to fluency in reading, but that such checks will inevitably occur on encountering words which are effectively those of a foreign language. Readers quite rightly feel, nevertheless, that they are entitled to what appears to be dialogue that is typically Scottish. To satisfy this feeling, therefore, the text has to be so manipulated as to impart to it no more than the *flavor* of Scottish speech at the same time as those readers are given the impression that this truly is the way a Scot would talk in any given circumstance. Running true, also, to the whole ethos of Scotland, one has to try in this to make a virtue out of necessity, in that dialogue of this kind can very often enhance a meaning and, instead of obscuring the text, can enrich it.

There is finally, on this question of problems to be faced, that of conveying to the young reader one's feeling for the values of one's native culture. And for that, the only solution to be found is also highly typical of writing from Scotland—that of characterizations powerful enough to be channels for these values. To create conflict between these characters and others strong enough to be their antitheses is to ensure that a theme will emerge; and just as surely then as night follows day, it is through that theme that those values will be demonstrated.

But to look finally at the broader aspects of writing from a minority culture, and moving to consider the theme as embracing now *any* minority culture, the question still to be asked is, "What benefits will this bring to young readers of countries other than those of the writers concerned?" That question applies, too, however small or however massive those countries may be in comparison to that of a writer's own. And again for answer to this I look back—in the first instance at least—to childhood days.

Of all the various books from other countries I encountered then, every single one was a total fascination to me simply *because* it came from a culture other than my own. But even more important than the exotica I gleaned from these books was the fact that they gave me my first opportunity to feel something about the *people* of the countries in which they were set.

The world, since that far-off time of my own childhood, has changed more rapidly in practical terms than in any century previous to our own. In my own lifetime, indeed—and I have not yet reached the Biblical span of threescore years and ten—it has gone from horse-drawn transport to that of the space age. For all practical purposes too, as transportation has become ever more speedy, the world has shrunk to what we now think of as a "global village." This, in turn, has created other aspects of change; yet, paradoxically, there is still one thing that remains constant.

The television pictures crossing frontiers that formerly were quite uncrossable have now made it impossible to hide from the people of any one country the events happening elsewhere. But just as there is a hunger everywhere for the news conveyed by such means, there is a hunger also to know something of the imaginative life of the people in countries other than one's own; and so the one thing that has not changed is the need—the need that has always existed—for fiction that can cross frontiers. Our whole world, indeed, has entered a period in which that need is more than ever evident; and, as always, its primary application is to children.

As others besides myself can testify from personal experience, after all, it is fiction more often than not that enables one to take the first step in feeling empathy with the people of another country. Additionally, to taste of their life through this medium, and to enjoy doing so, is to feel that one is being welcomed among them; and so what better way exists for creating understanding among those who are the most important among the peoples of our shrinking world—the children?

But, harking back to the writer's role in all this, there will still be many from various countries who wish to continue working in the non-English tongue of some minority culture, and yet would wish also to be read in the majority market primarily available only to English-language writers. So the problem of translation arises. And to what extent can this prevent the writer reaching the wider audience desired? This was the question put to me some years ago by Welsh writers trying to launch a scene of children's writing in their own language, and my reaction was to ask how many of them spoke Danish.

There's a high IQ among the Welsh! Everyone there made immediate connection between tiny Denmark with its minority language, and my oblique way of equating the possibilities of their situation with the fame achieved by Denmark's son, Hans Christian Andersen—the greatest of all children's writers.

In effect, as I went on in more explicit terms, it's not the source of the material, nor the tongue in which this is expressed that matters most in the end, but the quality of the writing; not the chances you're given that count, but what you do with these. As they say—and much more succinctly too—in theatrical circles, "There *are* no small parts—only small actors."

To sum up, then, on that same note. The geographical boundaries of Scotland are narrow, and its minority culture is a distinctive one. But the Scots themselves are a hospitable people; and for the writers among them—the children's writers especially—this should be yet another reason to add to those already dictating the aim of making that culture open and accessible to readers everywhere. What applies to them, also, applies equally to children's writers from every other minority culture, all of whom—like those Welsh writers who eventually *did* create an active scene in children's fiction—will come to realize there is no problem in this that cannot be overcome.

Technique will go part of the way in finding the needed solution. As for the rest, there are no boundaries to the imagination, any more than there ever should be to the heart.

ABOUT
THE AUTHOR

MOLLIE HUNTER is the author of many popular and acclaimed books for young people. She loves to write about the people of her native Scotland—from the distant history of THE STRONGHOLD, which won the 1974 Carnegie Medal (the British equivalent of the Newbery Medal), to recollections of her own young adult years, reflected in A SOUND OF CHARIOTS (winner of the 1992 Phoenix Award given by the Children's Literature Association to a book for children published twenty years earlier which, from the perspective of time, is deemed worthy of special recognition for its high literary quality) and its sequel HOLD ON TO LOVE. Her most recent book, THE MERMAID SUMMER, makes no mention of time or place but is steeped in the magic of the Scottish folklore tradition that Hunter knows so well. As one distinguished American critic proclaimed, she is "Scotland's most gifted storyteller."

In addition to her books for children, she has written several one-act plays, published in Great Britain, and articles on Scots history which have appeared in *The Glasgow Herald* and *The Scotsman*. In 1975 she was chosen to deliver the sixth annual May Hill Arbuthnot Honor Lecture at the University of Pennsylvania; it was this lecture that both inspired and formed the basis for TALENT IS NOT ENOUGH, a collection of lectures on writing for children.